ADVICE

TO A

YOUNG CHRISTIAN

ON THE
IMPORTANCE OF AIMING AT AN
ELEVATED STANDARD OF PIETY.

BY A VILLAGE PASTOR

WITH

AN INTRODUCTORY ESSAY

BY THE REV. DR. ALEXANDER, OF PRINCETON, N.J.

"Feed My Lambs"

Gospel Mission Press
1980

ORIGINALLY PRINTED IN 1830, REPRODUCED AND TYPESET BY GOSPEL MISSION IN 1980.

Distributed by
Gospel Mission International, Inc.
316 1st Ave., N. W.
P. O. Box M
Choteau, Montana 59422
Phone [406] 466-2311

Published by
Gospel Mission Press
402 South Main Street
Choteau, Montana 59422

— CONTENTS —

Introductory Essay	5
Letter I	29
Letter II	35
Letter III	40
Letter IV	46
Letter V	52
Letter VI	58
Letter VII	64
Letter VIII	70
Letter XI	75
Letter XII	81
Letter XIII	87
Letter XIV	92
Letter XV	97
Letter XVI	102
Letter XVII	108
Letter XVIII	113
Letter XIX	118
Letter XX	123
Letter XXI	128
Letter XXII	133
Letter XXIII	138
Letter XXIV	143
Letter XXV	148
Letter XXVI	153
Letter XXVII	158
Letter XXVIII	162
Conclusion	167

PREFACE

To the Lambs of Christ's flock, whom Peter was enjoined by the Good Shepherd to feed, I dedicate this little book. The letters which compose it, were written to instruct one of their number, the daughter of an highly valued friend. Since they are now made public, it is the ardent prayer of the Author, that they may comfort and edify many more.

As revivals of Religion have become so frequent, and have embraced in their sanctifying influence, so many youth of both sexes: these letters are given to the public, with the hope, that under God, they may stimulate such youth to activity in the cause of Christ; and awaken a desire for those exalted spiritual attainments, which it is their object to recommend.

The age in which we live, demands a high standard of Christian character. Any thing which contributes to elevate it, must be useful.

In presenting this little volume, the Author has no apologies to offer. Not that he supposes it free from defects, or impervious to the shafts of criticism; but because; if it is calculated to be useful, apologies are unnecessary; if it is not, none, however laboured or eloquent, can atone for so grand and radical a defect.

ESSAY

ON THE NATURE OF VITAL PIETY;—ITS SAMENESS IN ALL AGES AND COUNTRIES—AND ITS VARIOUS ASPECTS IN DIFFERENT CIRCUMSTANCES.

True religion not only enlightens the understanding, but rectifies the affections of the heart. All genuine feelings of piety are the effects of divine truth. The variety and intensity of these feelings depend on the different kinds of truth, and the various aspects in which the same truth is viewed; and also, on the distinctness and clearness with which it is presented to the mind. In a state of moral perfection, truth would uniformly produce all those emotions and affections which correspond with its nature, without the aid of any superadded influence. That these effects are not experienced, by all who have the opportunity of knowing the truth, is a strong evidence of human depravity. In a state of moral depravity, the mind is incapable alike, of perceiving and feeling the beauty and excellence of divine truth. The dead neither see nor feel, and man is by nature "dead in trespasses and sins." Hence the necessity of the agency of the Holy Spirit to illuminate and regenerate the mind. The nature of divine agency, in every case, is not understable by mortals. "The wind bloweth where it listeth, and thou hearest the sound thereof, but canst not tell whence it cometh, or whither it goeth: so is every one that is born of the Spirit." We know, however, that the work of the Spirit, in the regeneration of the heart, is adapted to the rational nature of man. The thing to be accomplished is not the creation of some new faculty; it is a moral renewing; and all moral changes must be effected by understanding and choice. To put the soul, therefore, in that state in which it will rightly understand the truth, and cordially choose the highest good, is the end of regeneration. Truth, therefore, must be the means by which actual conversion to God takes place. "Being born again, not of corruptible seed, but of incorruptible, by the word of God, which liveth and abideth for ever." "Of his own will begat he us with the word of truth." "Sanctify them through thy truth, thy word is truth." Although piety in the heart is the effect of a divine operation, yet all its exercises take place agreeably to the common laws of our rational nature. The understanding is enlightened, the judgment is convinced, motives operate on the will, and conscience approves or disapproves. That the soul, in the exercises of piety, is under the renewing influences of the Holy Spirit, is not known by any consciousness which it has of these divine operations, but by the effects produced in a change of views and feelings; and this change is ascribed to God, because no other is able to produce it; and his word assures us that he is its author.

Now, as all men are given the same natural sensibilities, and as all Christians contemplate the same fundamental truths, the work of grace in the hearts of all, must be substantially the same. All have, by the knowledge of the law, been convinced of sin; have been made to feel sorrow, shame, and guilt, upon the recollection of their transgressions; and to submit to the justice of the sentence of condemnation, which the law denounces against them. All have been made sensible of their own inability to save themselves, and under the influence of these humbling and penitent feelings, have been led to seek refuge in Jesus Christ, as the only hope of their souls. This plan of salvation appears glorious and suitable to all believers; so that they not only assent in it, as the only method of salvation, but they are so well pleased with it, that they would not have another if they could. And, in the acquaintance of Christ as a complete Saviour, there is, in every case, some experience of joy and peace. Connected with the views which the true believer has of Christ as a Saviour, there is also a discovery, more or less clear, of the glory of the divine attributes, especially of those which are especially manifested in the cross of Christ. Holiness, justice, mercy, and truth, shine, in the view of the sincere convert, with a lustre surpassing all other excellence; and God is respected and loved for his own glorious excellence, as well as for the rich benefits bestowed upon us. But, although these views may be distinguished, yet in experience, they are not separated. The brightest discovery of divine excellence ever made, is God's love to our miserable race. The law of God is also viewed to be holy, just, and good, by every regenerated soul. The unrenewed heart never is, nor ever can be, reconciled to the law; "it is not subject to it, nor indeed can be," but the "new man" delights in the law of God, and would not have one precept of it altered; and while it condemns all his feelings and works as imperfect, he approves of it still, and blames himself for his want of conformity to a rule so perfect.

Another thing in which the experience of all Christians is uniform, is that they all are brought to a deliberate purpose to be on the Lord's side. On this point there is no hesitancy. Many are affected, and much agitated with religious impressions, and yet never come to a full submission to follow God and his service. They halt between two opinions, and have a divided mind. Such persons, however lively their feelings, are not yet truly converted: all true converts, after counting the cost, have settled this point for ever. And they can say with the Psalmist, "My heart is fixed, O God, my heart is fixed." They are, therefore, prepared now to comply with the terms of discipleship laid down by Christ himself. They are willing to "deny themselves, to take up their cross, and follow him; to forsake father and mother, wife and children, houses and lands, yea also their own lives, for the sake of Him, who gave himself for them."

Out of such views and feelings as have been described, arises, an ardent hungering and thirsting after righteousness, an intense desire to know more of God, and to be admitted into closer union and more intimate communion with him. These habitual desires of the renewed soul, find their proper expression in prayer, and lead to a patient and earnest waiting upon God in all the ordinances and means of his appointment. True piety, however, does not stop in mere desires, or in attendance on religious duties; it seeks to glorify God by action. The earnest inquiry of every soul, inspired with the love of God, is, "Lord, what wouldst thou have me to do?" And wherever there is piety towards God, there will exist benevolence towards men. One of the most sensible emotions of the young convert, is, "goodwill to men;" a sincere desire of the welfare and eternal salvation of all, not even excepting its most deep-rooted enemies. And towards the children of God, there springs up a strong and tender affection. Such seem to be brethren indeed, because they are the brethren of Christ, and bear something of his image, in the humility, meekness, and benevolence of their character. In short, genuine piety disposes and determines all who are its subjects, to obey and respect all the commandments of God, and to hate and avoid all sin, according to that declaration of David, "I esteem all thy precepts concerning all things to be right, and hate every false way."

In all the above-mentioned essential characteristics of piety, there is a perfect sameness, in the exercises of all true Christians. The same impression has been made on every renewed heart, and the only difference is, that it is imprinted more deeply on some, than others; but still, the characters are identical; and, therefore, the evidences of a work of grace, contained in the Holy Scriptures, are equally applicable to all persons who have been brought from darkness to light. There often is, moreover, a striking resemblance in those accompanying exercises and circumstances, which are not essential. Awakened sinners are liable to the same erroneous conceptions, and usually fall into the same mistakes. They are all prone to think, that by reforming their lives they can restore themselves to the favour of God. They commonly apply to the works of the law for relief, in the first instance; and when driven from this false refuge, by a clearer view of the spirituality and extent of the law, and the depth of their own depravity, they are apt to give up all for lost, and seriously to conclude that there is no hope in their case. They are all prone to misunderstand the nature of the gospel: of its freeness they can at first form no conception; and, therefore, they think it necessary to come with some price in their hands—to obtain some kind of preparation or fitness, before they venture to come to Christ. And when it is clear that no moral fitness can be obtained, until they apply to him, this legal spirit will lead the soul under conviction to think, that very deep and sharp distress will recommend it to Christ; and thus many are found seeking and praying for a more deep and alarming impression of their sin and danger. It is also very common to place undue dependence on particular means; especially on such as have been much blessed to others. Anxious souls are prone to think, that in reading some particular book, or in hearing some successful preacher, they will receive the grace of God which bringeth salvation; in which expectation they are always disappointed, and are brought at last to feel that they are entirely dependent on sovereign grace; and that they can do nothing to obtain that grace. Before, they were like a drowning man catching at every thing which seemed to promise support; but now, they are like a man who feels that he has no support, but is actually sinking. Their cry, therefore, is now truly a cry for *mercy.* "God be merciful unto me a sinner!" "Lord save, I perish!" And it has often been said, "Man's distress is God's opportunity," which is commonly realized by the soul cut off from all dependence on itself—the arm of the Lord is stretched forth to preserve it from sinking; the Saviour's voice of love and mercy is heard; light breaks in upon the soul, and it finds itself embraced in the arms of the Saviour; and so wonderful is the change, that it can scarcely trust to its own experience.

This similarity of feelings in the experience of the pious has often been remarked, and has been justly considered a strong evidence of the divine origin of experimental religion: for how, otherwise, can this uniformity of the views and feelings of the pious, in all ages and countries, be accounted for? Enthusiasm assumes a thousand different shapes and is marked by no uniform characteristics; but scriptural piety is the same now, as in the days of David and Asaph; the same, as when Paul lived, the same, as experienced by the pious fathers of the Christian church; the same, as described by the Reformers, by the Puritans, and by the evangelical preachers and writers of the present day. When the gospel takes effect on any of the heathen, although it is certain that they never had the opportunity of learning any thing of this kind from others, yet we find them expressing the same feelings which are common to other Christians. Persons from different quarters of the globe, whose native tongue is entirely different, yet speak the same language in religion. Members of churches, which hold no communion; and which, perhaps, view each other, when at a distance as heretics, often, when brought together, recognize in one another dear brethren, who are of one mind in their religious experience.

The late eminently pious and learned theologian, the Rev. Dr. Livingston, related to me, not many years before his decease, a pleasant story, which will serve to illustrate the point under consideration; and which I communicate to the public the more willingly, because I do not know that he has left any record of it behind him. While a student at the university of Utrecht, a number of pious persons, from the town and from among the students, were accustomed to meet for free conversation on experimental religion, and for prayer and praise, in a social capacity. On one of these occasions, when the similarity of the exercises of the pious, in all countries and ages, was the subject of conversation, it was remarked by one of the company, that there was then present a representative from each of the four quarters of the world. These were Dr. Livingston from America, a young man from the Cape of Good Hope in Africa, another student from one of the Dutch possessions in the East Indies, and many natives of Europe of course. It was therefore proposed, that at the next meeting, the three young gentlemen first referred to, together with an eminently pious young nobleman of Holland, should each give a particular narrative of the rise and progress of the work of grace in his own soul. The proposal was universally acceptable; and accordingly, a narrative was heard from a native of each of the four quarters of the globe—of their views and feelings, of their trials and temptations, etc. The result was highly gratifying to all present; and I think Dr. Livingston said, that it was generally admitted by those present, that they had never before witnessed so interesting a scene. And since I have taken the liberty of mentioning the name of that distinguished theologian, I beg leave to add, that I have never seen a man who appeared to love vital piety more, or to understand its nature better.

But the identity of religious feeling which has been described above, is consistent with a great variety in many of the accompanying circumstances. Indeed, it seems probable, that each individual Christian has something distinctly characteristic in his own case; so that there exists, at least, as much difference in the peculiar features of the inner as of the outward man. The causes of these differences are manifold; as first, the different degrees of grace received, in the commencement of the divine life; secondly, the extent to which they have respectively run in sin, and the suddenness, or gradual nature of their change; thirdly, the degree of religious knowledge which is possessed; and finally, no small diversity arises from the various constitutional temperaments of different persons, which must have a powerful effect in giving complexion to the exercises of religion. To all which may be added, the manner in which persons under religious impressions are treated by their spiritual guides; and especially the manner in which the gospel is preached to them.

It has been remarked by men of exact observation, that particular revivals of religion are often marked by something peculiar in the exercises, and in the spirit of those who are the subjects of them. In some revivals, convictions are more sharp and awful, or continued for a longer time, than in others; and the converts, in some revivals, appear to acquire a much deeper and more abiding impression of the reality and glory of divine things, and are evidently more under the constraining influence of the love of Christ, than is observable in other cases. These are subjects which deserve a careful investigation; and as revivals are increasing in frequency and extent in our churches; and as different modes of conducting them are in use, it is highly important, that some man of deep experience, and sober, impartial judgment, should make observations extensively, and communicate them to the religious public; which is, in many places, perplexed and distracted, with the different methods of treatment recommended by different persons, and different parties. It may, however, be laid down as a sound rule, that in proportion as the truth of God is clearly brought to view, and faithfully applied to the heart and conscience, the good effects will be manifest. Erroneous opinions, although mingled with the essential truths of the gospel, will ever tend to mar the work of God. The good produced on any individual, or on a society, must not be judged of by the violence of the feelings excited, but by their character. Men may be consumed by a fiery zeal, and yet exhibit little of the meekness, humility, and sweet benevolence of Jesus. Great pretenders and high professors may be proud, arrogant, and critical. When these are the effects, we may, without fear, declare, "that they know not what manner of spirit they are of." Any religion, however corrupt, may have its zealots; but true Christianity consists in the fruits of the Spirit, which are "love, joy, peace, long suffering, gentleness, goodness, faith, meekness, temperance."

Piety seems also to assume an aspect somewhat different, in different ages and periods of the church. There is in human nature a strong tendency to run to extremes; and from one extreme, immediately to the opposite. And as the imperfections of our nature mingle with every thing which we touch, so piety itself is not exempt from the influence of the tendency above mentioned. In one age, or in one religious community, the leaning is to enthusiasm; in another, to superstition. At one time, religion is made to assume a severe and gloomy aspect; the conscience is gloomy and things indifferent are viewed as sins; and human infirmities are magnified into crimes. At such times, all cheerfulness is proscribed; and the Christian whom nature prompts to smile, feels a check from the conscience within. This value of genuine piety is also often connected with an unreasonable attitude. Now, when true religion is disfigured by such defects, it appears before the world to great disadvantage. Men of the world form their opinions of the nature of piety, from what they observe in its professors; and from such an exhibition of it as we have described, they often take up prejudices, which are never removed. There is, however, an opposite extreme, not less dangerous and injurious than this, when professors of religion conform to the world, so far that no clear distinction can be observed between the Christian and the worldling. If the former error drives men away from religion, as a sour and miserable thing, this leads them to the opinion, that Christians are activated by the same principles as they are; and therefore they conclude that no great change of their character is necessary. It is sometimes alleged by professors who thus accommodate themselves to the fashions and amusements of the world, that they hope by this means to render religion attractive, and thus gain over to piety those who neglect it; but this is a weak pretext, for such conformity always tends to confirm people in their carelessness. When they see professors at the theatre, or figuring in the ball-room, their conclusion either is, that there is no reality in vital piety, or that these professors act inconsistently.

The religious habits of some serious professors of religion, are apt to make a very unfavourable impression on the minds of sensible men. They assume a false piety, and speak in an affected and drawling tone; often sighing, and lifting up their eyes, and giving audible utterance to their own emotions. Now these persons may be, and I doubt not, often are, truly pious; but the impression made on most minds, by this affectation of religious solemnity, is, that they are hypocrites, who aim at being thought uncommonly devout. It appears to me, that religion never appears so lovely, as when she wears the dress of perfect simplicity. We ought not, indeed, to be ashamed of our religion, before the world; but it obligates us to be very careful, not to give to others an unfavourable opinion of serious piety. The rule is, "Let your light *so* shine that others seeing your good works may glorify your Father, who is in heaven." "Let not your good be evil spoken of."

But the aspect and character of the piety of one age, may differ from that of another, more from the peculiar circumstances in which Christians are placed, than from the preference of erroneous views or incorrect habits. In one age, vital piety seeks retirement, and runs in hidden channels. At such a time, the attention of Christians is turned chiefly on themselves. Much time is devoted to devotional exercises; often whole days. The secret recesses of the heart are explored with diligence and rigour; in-dwelling sin is detected in its many appearances, and is mortified with determined resolution; the various means of personal growth in grace are studied, and used with persevering diligence; and much useful knowledge of the nature of the spiritual life in the soul is acquired. But while vital piety is thus carefully cultivated, and the attention is earnestly turned to the exercises of the heart, there may be very little display of active, enlarged benevolence; there may be few vigorous efforts made to improve the condition of the multitudes perishing in sin. Under the influence of these defective views of the nature of religion, many pious persons, in the early ages of Christianity, withdrew entirely from the world, and lived in the wilderness; which mistake occasioned innumerable evils to the church, the effects of which are not yet corrected.

The spirit of piety among the Reformers, seems to have been pure and vigorous, but not as expansive as it might have been. They seem scarcely to have thought of the hundreds of millions of heathens in the world; and of course, made no efforts to extend the knowledge of salvation to them. Indeed, they were so much occupied at home, in contending for the faith against the Romanists, that they had little time left evangelizing at a distance; but if that zeal which was worse than wasted in controversy with one another, had been directed to the coversion of the heathen, their usefulness would have been far greater than it was.

The Puritans also, although profoundly acquainted with experimental religion, seemed to have confined their attention too exclusively to themselves. Their ministers were, it is true, silenced, and driven into corners and into exile, by an ungrateful and cruel government; but it seems wonderful to us, that when prevented from preaching the gospel to their own countrymen, they did not turn to the gentiles. But the era of missions had not yet arrived, and probably they had but small opportunity, in their persecuted state, of uniting their counsels of combining their energies in schemes of distant benevolence. One thing, however, is now manifest, that the providence of God overruled the retirement and leisure of those godly ministers, who were ejected from their charges, so as to render their labours more useful to the church, than if they had been permitted to spend their lives in preaching the gospel; for, when deprived of the liberty of employing their tongues, they betook themselves to their pens, and they have left to the church such a body of practical and convicting theology, as all ages before or since, cannot equal. I have no doubt, that such men as Owen, Baxter, Flavel, Bunyan, Goodwin, Manton, Howe, and Bates, have effected much more good by their practical writings, than they could possibly have done by their preaching, supposing them to have been ever so successful.

But our lot is cast in a different age, and in a different state of the church. After a long slumber, the attention of Christians has been aroused to consider the perishing condition of the heathen. We live in a period when great designs are entertained, and plans formed for the conversion of the whole world,—when one benevolent enterprise or institution follows another in rapid succession, until the Christian community begins to exhibit an entirely new aspect, from what it did within our own remembrance. Christians have begun to feel, that by a combination of effort, they have power to accomplish much. The public attention is kept awake by the frequent recurrence of public meetings of an interesting kind, and by that more potent engine, the wide circulation of religious PERIODICALS, by which, interesting intelligence is conveyed to almost every corner of our extensive country. The duty of Christians to be active is now taught, in almost every form; tracts are multiplied; the scriptures are circulated; the young and ignorant are instructed, by new methods; and many are found running to and fro to promote the distribution of evangelical truth. Revivals of religion also are exerting a mighty influence on the church. The number of serious Christians is vastly increased; and many youth are brought forward to a course of preparation for the gospel ministry. A spirit of liberality also is witnessed, unknown to our fathers; and the duty of consecrating to the Lord, a reasonable proportion of all their increase, is beginning to be extensively felt among serious Christians. And such is the spirit of enterprise, that no undertaking appears too difficult, which has for its object the advancement of the Redeemer's kingdom: and such is the favour of heaven towards benevolent enterprises in our day, that scarcely one has failed of accomplishing some good; and although the schemes of benevolence are so various and so multiplied, yet there has occurred no sensible interference of one with another. As they all aim at the same object, so they are all viewed as parts of the same great system of operations. Now, in all these favourable appearances and benevolent exertions, every pious heart must and will rejoice.

But is there no danger, that many who feel interested in the operations of the day, and contribute to their advancement, should be mistaken as to their true spiritual condition? When a powerful current takes a set, many will be carried along with it, which ever way it may run. And is there no danger that Christians themselves, while they seem to flourish in external profession, zeal and activity, may be decaying at the root, for want of sufficient attention to their own hearts, and to the duties of the closet? There is indeed much reason to fear that many professors now exist, who confine their religion too much to those external acts, which may be performed from motives no higher than those which operate on unrenewed men. The danger now is, that the religion of the heart will be neglected, and that many will feel well satisfied with themselves, on account of their activity and zeal, who are yet strangers to a work of grace. This being the point on which Christians of the present day are liable to err, it is a matter of congratulation, that some writers seem disposed to turn the attention of the Christian public, to the importance of diligence and punctuality in performing the duties of the closet. The following letters are well calculated to produce this effect. They were forwarded to me by an esteemed young clergyman, who is settled as a pastor in a distant and retired village. They were addressed, as the author has stated in his preface, to a young lady of highly respectable connexions, upon the occasion of her making a public profession of religion. The father of this young lady, who is distinguished for his benevolence and evangelical piety, was unwilling that the pious and judicious counsels and affectionate exhortations which they contain should be limited to an individual, since they are so well adapted to be useful to Christians generally; and especially to the young, placed in circumstances similar to those of the person to whom they were originally addressed. A request was, therefore, made for their publication. The author through modesty has withheld his name, but has requested me to introduce them to the public with some preliminary essay of my own; with which request I have here complied, believing that the letters of my young friend are seasonable, judicious, and pious, and that as they are written in an interesting and lively style, they will be extensively perused by the young.   **A. ALEXANDER.**

Princeton, N. J.

ADVICE, &c.
LETTER I.

DEAR YOUNG FRIEND,

You are very young to profess the high character of a Christian; but your youth, while it serves as a caution, should not operate as a discouragement. Many a person of fewer years, and with less advantages, has not only given satisfactory evidence of conversion, but proved, in subsequent life, to be of that number whose "path shineth more and more, unto the perfect day."

It becomes you, however, to look narrowly into the evidences of such a change. A mistake here will prove fatal. The word of God and prayer, are the great means, which, if faithfully applied, will in due time, develop your true moral character. If you have been deceived, if yet in your sins, these duties will ere long become irksome, and be loosely performed or utterly neglected. If you have been regenerated, you will not only persevere in these duties, but will find that they produce more and more of your interest, until you arrive at a well-grounded hope of eternal joy.

Taking for granted, that you do not make this profession on slight grounds, nor with inadequate or erroneous views; my object, in a few letters which I shall address to you, will be to urge you to the formation of an elevated Christian character. You profess to have taken the first step in the straight and narrow way; but recollect, it is *only* the first step. The concentrated gaze of many eyes is upon you. Some would exult in your downfall—others rejoice in your advancement. Invisible and wicked spirits will tempt you to ruin. Good and guardian angels will watch around your steps, and rejoice in your victories. To sustain *yourself,* you have already been convinced is impossible. If you are regenerated, you are not perfectly sanctified; nor *will* you be, until death shall be swallowed up in victory. But as Paul could do all things, by the strength of his master, so can the weakest believer; and you must ever feel that the same grace, which brought "you out of nature's darkness," must enable you to overcome your enemies, and "persevere unto the end."

As I have touched upon this point, I am forcibly reminded of the beautiful dream of the Rev. John Newton, while lying at anchor in the harbour of Venice, and within sight of a part of the Alps. For the particulars, I refer you to his volumes. The substance is as follows:

The anxiety of mind which he endured in his waking hours, seemed to give a colouring to his night vision. He felt himself in great confusion and horror. While musing on the wretchedness of his condition, there appeared suddenly, a heavenly figure, who presented to him a ring, which she said, if preserved with care, would, on every difficult occasion, resolve his doubts, and deliver him from trouble. He was overjoyed at the reception of it. All his fears seemed to subside, and a heavenly serenity to succeed. While in this tranquil and happy frame of mind, another personage, of less inviting aspect, made his appearance, and, after many flattering words and artful insinuations, prevailed on him to part with the ring. He deliberately dropped it over the side of the vessel, and it sunk to the bottom. The flames, in an awful manner, immediately burst from the mountain, and he seemed threatened with instant destruction. At this moment of horror, his celestial friend again appeared, and, with a frown of mingled love and reproof, upbraided him for listening to the voice of the tempter. She then descended into the water, and soon returned bearing the ring, and thus addressed him: "As thou art unable to keep this token, I will preserve it for thee, and it shall be secure for ever."

I have only given you from memory an outline of this beautiful vision. The interpretation, which the author put upon it, is full of spiritual instruction. If left for one moment to our own strength, how soon do we abandon the "ring," even at the first suggestion of the tempter! Then the soul is affrighted and dismayed. But Jesus, our guardian, is able to restore the "ring," and lest we should lose it, he, in condescension to our infirmities, consents to keep it. "I will never leave thee, nor forsake thee," is his language. Thus, my dear young friend, entrust the "ring" to Him, who alone is able to preserve it. When the tempter comes, whether in the artful guise of what the world calls innocent pleasure, or the bold assaults of blasphemy and despair, look upward to Him who is charged with the care of all that is precious to the soul. Wait not until you are overwhelmed by the consciousness of contracted guilt, but flee—oh flee, as for your life, to Jesus! You cannot trust him too confidently. He will permit you to sit even at his feet. There is honour, there is safety, there is happiness.

I congratulate you, on the favourable circumstances in which you are placed for the formation of Christian character. The work of divine grace in which you profess to be a participant, is, I understand, still in progress. Doubtless you find some kindred spirits with whom you can mingle feelings, unite in mutual prayer, and converse on the sweetest of all topics, the love of your Lord and Master. Let it be a principle with you, to select as your companions, the most heavenly-minded of your sex. If such can be found in the higher walks of life, very well; be they your bosom friends; but, alas! how seldom, in the higher circles, does religion, in its native simplicity and purity, appear! You must seek it, I apprehend, in the low vale of darkness, and often amid the homely attire of honest poverty. If you have the spirit of Christ, you will love his image, though arrayed in an humble garb. I know it has ever been the design of your parents, to make you estimate character, not by riches, nor fashionable appearance, but by real moral worth; and I am persuaded that you must now feel, that if Providence has given you advantages of wealth and education, above the average person, it is a ground of humility, in as much as it lays you under the greater obligations. Where "much is given," oh, never forget it! "much will be required." On this principle, are you not bound to be humble, benevolent, condescending?

In closing this letter, I must say to you as I lately said to a youth in my parish, who is about making a public profession of her faith in Christ: "I hope you will not be satisfied with being half a Christian." So, my young friend, I would exhort you to aim high. It is a day to elevate the standard of piety. We want more Newels, and Huntingtons, and Ramsays, and Smelts. These were devoted souls. It was not half-way work with them. Religion was "all in all." For this they lived—they suffered—and, supported by its consolations, they died. They have left a bright track for you to follow. Tread closely in their steps; and then, though you share in their sufferings, you shall also inherit, with them, the "crown of glory."

LETTER II.

AMONG the first temptations which you will probably experience, will be an effort, on the part of your spiritual enemies, to deceive you back to the pleasures of the world. Sometimes it will be a direct and powerful attack. The ways of religion will be represented as difficult, whilst those of worldly pleasure will be strewed with flowers. "What," the tempter will exclaim, "shall one so young, so susceptible of enjoyment from all the varied delights of sense—one who has it in her power to command almost any imaginable happiness—shall she put on the grave aspect of piety and thus debar herself from every innocent pleasure? Look abroad, see thy young companions, how their hearts beat with rapture, as they float amid the circles of beauty and of fashion. Why shouldst thou become a sober religionist, when thou art ripening for so much bliss?" In such false and flattering colours, will the tempter array the world. Knowing that vanity is one of the strongest principles of our depraved nature, he will constantly, and often successfully, appeal to it. His flatteries will respect your person, your accomplishments, your fortune. He will suggest that with such advantages, the world must pay you homage, and become a sort of perpetual paradise.

Had you, my young friend, been one of pleasure's gay devotees, as *I* have been, he could not, and probably he would not, thus address you. I could say, from experience—thou seducing spirit, what thou sayest is false. Have I not mingled in the festival? Have I not courted pleasure in the brilliant assembly, and the crowded theatre, where beauty and wealth have poured around their shining and fascinating attractions? And what did I ever gain? A momentary rapture, I admit; an uplifting of spirits, and a temporary forgetting of my cares. But this was all. And even these fleeting joys were not reduced. Jealousy, and envy, and hatred, and disappointment, would occasionally let fall the bitter drop, as the cup was passing to the lip; and disgust, and self-loathing, would succeed. But conscience was more powerful than all. What restless hours of wakeful solicitude, what anticipated wrath, what vain resolutions, what unavailing regrets! And shall the tempter tell me, that the pleasures of the world are worthy to be preferred to the calm delight of communion with God, and the high enjoyment of religion? "He was a liar from the beginning," and when, my young Christian friend, he assaults you with such suggestions, or when, through his agents in human form, he would seduce you from your allegiance, recollect his character, resist his suggestions—and, according to the promise, "he will flee from you."

But it is far more probable, that his insinuations will be almost unrecognized. A direct and powerful attack may throw a Christian on his face, and overwhelm him with agony; but Judah's lion shall appear, and affright the bold adversary. It is when your spiritual enemies are making a gradual advance on your purity and devotedness, that they are most to be dreaded, as most likely to be successful. Now, you are, I trust, conscientious in the discharge of the duty of private devotion. You love to retire from human observation, to commune with God. I would believe, that you are never so happy as when thus engaged; that you have a consecrated spot, which you call your Bethel, where the soul daily drinks in the waters of life.

Happy, dear youth, happy will you be, if that Bethel is always thus attractive and interesting. But the great danger is, that it will be neglected, and perhaps forsaken. You are ready to exclaim, "impossible! I shall never cease to pray. I could sooner dispense with my daily food, than forego the privileges of a throne of grace." This is the language of sincerity, I doubt not. You verily think so; but how little do you know the temptations which surround you, and the deceitfulness of your own heart? You have much to fear.

When called myself from nature's darkness, and made, as I hope, to taste the sweetness of redeeming love, I was of the same opinion. I had waked up in a new world. 'Twas as if the Creator had formed a new being, akin to the happy spirits in heaven, and dropped him on the earth, in the spring time of nature's magnificence and beauty. The foliage seemed greener and fresher than ever. The dew-drops glittered more brilliantly; the sky looked purer; and every thing seemed to shine and save, in silent but emphatic praise of God, their Creator. My soul beat in happy unison with these silent worshippers, and methought I could never cease to sing and pray. My very being seemed to consist in it. But has it been so ever since? Oh ye hours of anguish, ye days of carnality — ambition — and folly; ye can say how guilty, how careless, how ungrateful,

I have been. Little did I then dream of loving and serving the world. I thought I could have spent an eternity of happiness, on some lonely rock in the ocean, if God were with me there. I thought my soul would never forsake him, nor my voice ever be silent in his praise. But I knew not my own heart, nor the power of the world's allurements.

Now do not suppose, that because I and others have been tempted to backslide, and have yielded to the temptation, you must necessarily follow our disgraceful defection. I hope you never will. If you are a child of God, you need not. You may go "from strength to strength." You may accomplish victory after victory. God grant that you may!

But, should you, by mournful experience, have to look upon yourself as a backslider, you will remember this warning, and wish you had heeded it. Like the prodigal, you will be in spiritual beggary. I know of no condition, except that of hardened rebellion, more pitiable than the condition of a backslider. Conscience is too quick to allow him to enjoy the world; and religion is too much neglected to yield him the smallest comfort. He lives in disquietude, and anguish, until he repents, and finds anew the favour of his God.

LETTER III.

IN my last, I touched upon the subject of temptation. I am constrained to add a few words more on the same subject. It has been too common for those who have betrayed their Lord by a disgraceful return to the world, to predict the same defection in others. Hence you often hear professors of religion address the youthful convert in such language as the following: "Your present ardour is no proof that it will continue; now you are all joy, all devotion; by and by the scene will be changed. I once felt as you now feel; perhaps I enjoyed more delightful pleasure: but I soon lost the glow of my first love, and so will you. A few years will cool you down, and show you that such engagedness cannot always last."

When I hear such language addressed to the young Christian, I am indignant. It is not necessarily true; my young friend, it is not true. The Bible, which is the only "lamp to our path," gives no warrant for such a prediction. True, it represents the cases of many who at first bade fair, but subsequently hardened. It records the cases of such, as a flaming beacon, to warn those who should come after them. But does it not represent the path of the just, as "the shining light, which shineth more and more unto the perfect day?" Does it not say, that he who hath clean hands, shall grow "stronger and stronger?" Does it not urge us to "grow in grace," to "forget the things which are behind," and "reach towards those which are before?" to make Christ our mark, and press towards it, with all the energy of an Olympic racer, struggling in competition for the goal?

Now, I warn you not to listen to such cold predictions. They who make them from their own experience, may have been hypocrites. They may have felt something, which they called spiritual joy; but perhaps it was "Satan transformed into an angel of light:" perhaps it was the workings of their own imaginations, and not the legitimate fruits of the spirit. Let them take heed to themselves, lest they have been deceived; and not allure others on, in their down-hill course, by their disgraceful example. But suppose them to have been Christians; and I allow that a Christian may grow cold, and backslide in the service of God; is such language warranted by the word of God?

Is it likely to urge forward the young convert in the path of holiness? Is it likely to raise the standard of piety in the souls of others? No, far from it. Young converts are prone to copy those who are older and more experienced. If they are persuaded that it is consistent with the existence of piety, to grow cold in feeling, they will probably yield to the seductions of the world, and the temptations of Satan. They will not press forward; they will recede. They will take the cold dead level of their previous examples.

But, my young friend, be you warned by this, not to listen to such language for a moment; nor to suppose it must be true in your case. I do assure you, your Bible holds a different language. As you value your comfort, your peace of mind, your immortal hopes, your character as a Christian, your influence as a follower of the Lamb—press forward. Strive every day to make some new attainments in knowledge and holiness. You are engaged in a conflict. You have put on the armour of God; and, put it off for a moment you must not. Your enemies are numerous, vigilant, and powerful. You must contend every day: nor must you think of rest or relaxation. When death shall unbind for you the gospel armour, and you hear the dark waves of Jordan lashing these mortal shores, then, and not till then, will your struggles be ended, and your victory complete. You have counted the cost; do not shrink at the cross. Christ will be with you. Christ will support you. Under His banner you contend. His arm will shield you, and his grace bring you off more than conqueror.

I have wandered a little from the point at which I aimed. I wished to caution you particularly, concerning the first step in a backward course. The first step in the retreat is an important one. It is needful, therefore, to say, that generally, that step commences at the closet. Prayer is the strong hold to which the young Christian generally resorts. In doubts and difficulties, a throne of grace is his refuge. If the "devouring lion" roar, thither the lamb will flee, and house itself in the bosom of its shepherd. If the world entice, and for a moment soils his purity, thither he repairs, and the stain is washed out in the blood of Jesus. If the path of duty be not obvious, if confusion attend his course, at a throne of grace there is light and direction. Hence it will be an important advantage to your enemies, if they can draw you from this strong tower of defence. Keep alive then, I beseech you, to the first symptom of declining in prayer. Prayer is a difficult, strenuous work; but it is the life and soul of a Christian. It is not only His mandatory duty, but His most precious privilege.

Now it will be the aim of the tempter, to withdraw you from being "instant in prayer." He knows what a powerful weapon it is; and, therefore, he will endeavour to wrest it out of your hands. He will represent it as an irksome duty. He will suggest that fewer and shorter prayers will answer. He will place obstacles between you and your closet. He will divert your attention while there, and then taunt you with your coldness and your folly. He will say that your prayers are hypocritical—insincere—an abomination to God. He will suggest, that now, you are not in a good frame—advise you to put it off until you feel in a better. Thus will he try every art, and use every scheme to draw you form this refuge of your soul. But, "get thee behind me, Satan" must be your reply to all such suggestions. You must cling closer to the "horns of the altar." You must "bind the sacrifice with cords," if you cannot keep it there. You must give yourself to prayer, and to the word of God.

LETTER IV.

I FEEL constrained, my young friend, to add something more on the subject of prayer. This duty, in my view, is of such importance as to warrant a few more remarks; although I do not intend enlarging on a subject upon which so much, and such excellent things have been written.

You were taught, by your pious parents, to utter a form of prayer, as soon as your infant mind could comprehend, and your infant tongue able to utter a sentence. In looking back upon these juvenile devotions, you doubtless see wherein they were lacking. Your ideas of the Being to whom they were addressed, were confused and inadequate. You could not then comprehend the necessity of a Mediator; for as yet you had not discovered the evil of sin, and the wrath of God, as revealed against it. You had too deep a sense of obligation, to neglect prayer entirely; but of the real nature and effect of prayer, you had little conception. To your mind, prayer was a form of words to be repeated at stated intervals. When thus repeated, the obligation was discharged. This was probably all you knew about prayer.

But shall parents omit to impress this duty on their children, because they cannot comprehend the nature of it? Certainly not. How can they tell but that when they have taught the little toddler to compose himself to rest, with his familiar and simple petitions, the Spirit of God may enlighten the child into the spiritual import of his prayer, and make it a means of leading him to more enlarged petitions, offered up "in spirit and in truth." No person can estimate the advantages of early instruction of youthful mind with a sense of its obligations to God. Such instructions should commence with the first dawn of understanding and sure I am, that in subsequent life, the subject of them will generally be the better and the happier.

To illustrate this, I will refer again to my own case. I was taught by one of the best of mothers, never to close my eyes without repeating my prayers. This I conscientiously adhered to, until about thirteen or fourteen years of age, when I began gradually to omit them. Whether I felt that they were too childish, or whether, as is most probable, my conscience was becoming seared in the downhill course of iniquity, I cannot now remember. But at all events, my prayers were no longer offered; and I went to sleep and rose up like a brute. With the omission of these prayers, commenced a backsliding movement in morals, until I hung over the edge of ruin, ripe for the judgments of God. And what do you suppose occurred first, to rouse me from the fatal slumbers of death? As I was retiring one night, the recollection of my former punctual attention to prayer, rushed upon my mind. I paused. "What," said I to myself, "am I going to lie down without one thought of God, or offering one prayer for the safety of my soul? Did I not once repeat my prayers; and at a time too when I was far less guilty than now? Why have I omitted them so long? Suppose I should die this night, where then would my soul be?" With such reflections I became impressed; and although I did not kneel that night, yet in a relaxed posture, I began again to repeat my juvenile devotions. I was nearly seventeen years of age when I resumed them. I had almost forgotten them. A few days and nights rolled away, and convictions grew heavier on my soul. I thought a repetition of these forms was not enough. My soul began to sink in the deep waters; and a few more days brought me on my knees at the bed-side, with the prayer of the publican: "God be merciful to me a sinner."

Thus, my young friend, were my mother's early instructions, among the means, under God, of rescuing me from ruin, temporal and eternal. Thus it is evident, that the sooner children are taught to pray, the better; and no attention can be too great, to impress on them the obligation and the necessity of prayer.

Still I believe, that the Christian only, prays the acceptable prayer. Until the spirit of God convince of sin, the soul will not see its filthiness, nor pray for its removal. The danger to which it is exposed here and hereafter, it may see; and it may disapprove the punishment to which it is subjected; but it is only when the soul is renewed in the image of God, that "sin appears exceeding sinful," and that the effectual fervent prayer for sanctification is offered.

If you are a Christian, my young friend, the throne of grace is yours. Your Father is seated on it. Your Saviour has sprinkled it with his blood. The Holy Spirit draws you sweetly to kneel before it; and the promise, when there, is, "open your mouth wide, and I will fill it." What an honour thus to approach the King of kings! Were we to have audience with an earthly monarch, we should deem it an era in our history, and boast of it through life. But you, and I, and others, may have audience with the King of the universe. Nay, we have liberty to approach Him at any time, and under all circumstances. Have we wants, He can supply them. Are we in trouble, He can deliver us. Do afflictions press our souls, He can soften and remove them. Does sin pollute our joys, with Him is the fountain of cleansing. Does Satan vex our souls, He invites us to his arms as our refuge. All relief and every blessing is with God.

There is nothing which so elevates a character, and especially a female character, as deep and intimate communion with God. She seems then to be allied to angelic natures. A sort of mellow radiance is poured into her character, as if some particles of heaven's glory had been let fall upon her. She moves in a higher sphere than the generality of her sex. She is another being than those idle, sickly daughters of pleasure, who waste their lives in dreaming fanciful vision of happiness, sporting awhile amid life's tumultuous joys, and then sinking unblessed into a wretched eternity. She converses with God. At a throne of grace, she acquires a kindness, a dignity, a humility, which throw around her an attractive lustre, put sweetness into every action and expression, make her contented in every condition of life, patient under every affliction, faithful in the discharge of every duty, and which even grace her dying hours, and make her "death-bed privileged beyond the common walks of life."

LETTER V.

There are three inquiries, my young friend, respecting prayer, which every conscientious Christian will be likely to institute. How ought I to pray, when, or at what times, and for what things? These are important inquiries. A full and satisfactory answer, I feel myself unable to give. I shall, in my own poor way, barely touch upon each.

Those who worship God, are bound to "worship him in spirit and in truth." In spirit, as opposed to the mere external ceremonies. The Jews and Samaritans, at the time our Lord uttered the prediction just alluded to, were reposing an unfounded confidence in the mere forms and ceremonies of their religion; while in the expressive language of inspiration, their "hearts were far from God."

We must pray then with the Spirit. The heart must be in the work, or it will be insincere and ineffectual. The Quakers, you know, reject all external forms. They are on one extreme. The Jews and Catholics, having a multitude of forms, are on the other. I would not insinuate, that among Quakers and Catholics, there are no sincere worshippers; far from it. I believe there are many devout Christians among both. I am persuaded for my own part, that some attention to form and circumstance is an important auxiliary to us poor weak mortals, in our attempts to worship God. In my own experience I have found the benefit of it. For example; when I have a particular room allotted to my devotions—a certain place in that room, where I am accustomed to kneel—a degree of obscurity shed over the place by the exclusion of too great a glare of light; all these circumstances are a help to me, by the power of mental association. There is nature in this: and God permits us to have recourse to every lawful auxiliary in worshipping him. The great point is, to worship "in spirit and in truth."

True worship is distinguished from false, inas-much as the one is scriptural, but the other is not. A true worshipper views the character of God as it is described in the Bible. The omniscience, omnipresence, holiness, justice, goodness, and truth, of God, are attributes of delightful contemplation; and centering in one eternal, unchangeable, and incomprehensible Spirit, they excite his reverence, his confidence, his humility, and his love. He looks into his Bible to learn the character of God; and, as there found, worships him in spirit and in truth.

But can a guilty creature, who has violated every obligation he is under to his Creator, approach him without the intercession of a Mediator? I bring this question home to myself, and inquire, would I dare, as a supplicant, to approach my God and my Creator, in all my uncovered, aggravated guilt? This, my young friend, is the hinge of salvation. The Socinian, who does not believe in Deity or Trinity, will tell me, certainly you may. But my own conscience would give a different verdict. I see nought in my life but sin; sin of the most aggravated kind: I repeat these sins, and confess them; and again repeat them. Now, I say, is God holy? Is He opposed to sin? Then must I fall under His wrath and curse. Then how can I expect to escape His indignation? He is merciful, says the Socinian. True, he *is* merciful; but is not that mercy exercised in a peculiar way? Is it indiscriminate, unconditional mercy? Must not something be done to show God's abhorrence of my sins? Must not some sacrifice be made? Now I am brought to the delightful, soul-cheering feature of the Gospel: "God in *Christ*, reconciling the world unto Himself, not imputing their trespasses unto them." "He so loved the world, that he gave his only begotten Son, that whosoever believeth in Him should not perish, but have everlasting life." "He was wounded for our transgressions." On this foundation, my soul finds firm footing, and I rest secure in the promise of eternal life. Whosoever cometh unto the Father, therefore, must come through Christ; and so coming, shall not be cast out.

All acceptable prayer, is rendered so, by the merits and intercession of the Divine Saviour. He is our merciful and faithful High Priest. His own blood was shed for the remission of our sins: and the apostle says, "if any man sin, we have an advocate with the Father, Jesus Christ the righteous." When you pray, therefore, never lose sight of the Mediator. "His name is like ointment poured forth." The sinner's friend, he pleads the sinner's cause. He knows your infirmities, your temptations, and your trials, and is ever ready to afford you relief.

The doctrine of the Trinity is, I know, offensive to many, who are governed more by carnal reason, than by scripture; but to me, if I am not deceived, it is one of the most comforting, cheering, and elevating truths of the

Bible. I see the persons of the Godhead harmoniously engaged in my deliverance. In prayer, the Spirit seems to lift my lagging affections, and to carry them upward, pouring light into the dark chambers of the mind. Jesus, the Mediator, pleads my cause, even when my own tongue is dumb with grief, and my soul overwhelmed with conscious guilt. Then the throne of grace is precious, and the soul is replenished as with marrow and fatness.

I pity those whose scepticism has blotted out the glory of our Immanuel. Their religion is cold. It warms not the heart; it pacifies not the conscience; it prompts to few acts of self-denial; it almost erases the line between the righteous and the wicked; and it makes retribution ridiculous. After all, it is only a substitute, and a very poor one, for the glorious Gospel of the Son of God.

Having been heedlessly led, by the subject, to these remarks, I must now return. In prayer, we must be earnest—we must be sincere—we must have faith in the promises. The "fervent prayer availeth much." "Jacob wrestled;" what a strong expression! Jesus, in prayer, sweat drops of blood. Paul prayed with tears. Hannah wept at the altar. All these examples, and numerous others, such as the widow pleading with the unjust judge, show the necessity of earnestness in prayer. This I know is often difficult. You will come to the mercy-seat, with a cold heart and wandering thoughts; and how at such times can you be fervent? "The Spirit helpeth our infirmities," is the only repy I can offer. And this is sufficient. In such a frame of mind, there is the greater need of earnestness. Tarry not until your thoughts take a more elevated and spiritual tone. I have always found, that the best way of proceeding in such a case, was to apply immediately to a throne of grace. There wrestle; renew the supplication, and still renew it; until, as is often the case, the fire of heaven descends, and the sacrifice is enkindled. The Lord give you the spirit and the success of the patriarch Jacob.

LETTER VI.

Sincerity, my dear young friend, is an essential ingredient in prayer. Without it, no prayer can be acceptable. Indeed, if we are insincere, we cannot be said to pray. A mere form of words, is not prayer.

Prayer, is the desire of the heart for something which we judge to be necessary or beneficial. It implies a knowledge of our wants, and an urgent wish to have them supplied. If, therefore, the heart be roving after one object, while the lips are employed in asking for another, we are insincere and unacceptable worshippers. Such conduct is an insult to our Creator—a game of deception on ourselves. Such were the petitions at which God, in old times, declared himself indignant; when his professing people drew "nigh unto Him with their mouth, and honoured Him with their lips, while their heart was far from Him." Such was the religion of the Scribes and Pharisees; fair and beautiful without, but within, all rottenness and corruption.

Reflect a moment ere you bend the knee at the throne of grace. I am not now about to approach an earthly monarch, who, though surrounded with the pomp and circumstance of royalty, is but a worm of the dust like myself; but I am to have audience with the King of kings—the Lord of the whole earth. I am about to come into the presence, and to utter the name of Him, at whose command all creation sprang into existence. Were I in the presence of a finite being, I might perhaps conceal my feelings under a form of words. I might utter one thing and mean another. But can I thus practice deception with God? Are not all things "naked, and opened unto the eyes of Him, with whom we have to do?" Does not He search the hearts of the children of men? Will he be satisfied with any thing but "truth in the inward parts?" "If I regard iniquity in my heart," says the sweet singer of Israel, "the Lord will not hear me." And again, in his bold and beautiful questioning: "He that formed the eye, shall He not see? He that created the ear, shall He not hear?"

Let such be your meditation, when you are about to kneel at the throne of grace. Not that I would array the character of God in terrors to your mind, or send you to tremble like a slave at his feet. No, he is a God of love, of compassion. of long forbearance; more merciful and tender than the kindest earthly parent. You may go to Him, and you must so go, in the confiding simplicity of a child and a favourite. When you take to Him the name of Christ your Mediator, you take, so to speak, a passport into his very bosom. You may unburden your whole heart; tell Him things which you could confide to no mortal ear; make confession of sins, which you dare only whisper in your closet; and in the open frankness of faith and penitence, humbly cast yourself on his all-supporting arm. He is your covenant God; and, when alone with Him, you may indulge even a holy familiarity.

Reflect on your own character, as well as on that of the Being whom you address; the thought of both will humble you in the dust, and prepare you, in your approach to the mercy-seat, to appreciate the all-glorious, divine, and compassionate Mediator. Be careful to inquire into your wants. Say within yourself, why have I now retired? What errand have I at the throne? what sins to confess, what mercies to acknowledge, what wants to be supplied? For whom, beside myself, should I pray? what temptations appear to be most formidable? Let me not cover one sin, nor keep back one confession. Let me not ask for holiness, if I would retain a single lust; if I am not resolved to crucify all. Let me not ask for a revival of religion, if I do not secretly and sincerely wish for it. "Search me, O God, and know my heart; and see if there be any wicked way in me, and lead me in the way everlasting;" should ever be your wish and your petition. Let your sincerity be such, that you can ever thus appeal to the heart-searching God. Nothing is so well calculated to foster the spirit of devotion, as to be enabled to say with Peter, "thou knowest;" to make the familiar appeal, although I cannot, by reason of infirmity, express the number and aggravation of my sins, yet, oh Lord, "thou knowest," I lament them, and sincerely desire their removal; although my words fail in expressing my gratitude, yet "thou knowest," my heart is full; although I cannot give expression to my feeling in behalf of Zion, yet "thou knowest," I love her prosperity, and earnestly desire her increase and glory. "Thou knowest," is a sweet expression in the ears of a prayer-hearing God. It gives the soul a confidence and an earnestness, when pleading for itself, or for others.

You will find, my young friend, strong temptations to be shallow and hurried in your prayers. Your enemies will suggest some engagements which will cut short your supplications. They will insinuate, that all this meditation is unnecessary. If in these attacks they prevail, you will immediately perceive an insincerity in your prayers. You will find yourself, at times, wishing the prayer was over; and uttering it, rather as a sedative to conscience, than as the supreme delight of your soul. You will then, indeed, come like a slave to the altar; and, having performed to conscience, as to a stubborn tyrant, the accustomed task, you will be glad of a speedy relief. You may even find yourself, at times, uttering words and forms, of the meaning of which, while your heart is wandering on forbidden objects, you are totally unconscious. This is sinful in the extreme.

May you never arrive at this melancholy pitch of insult, and of mockery!

Yield not, dear young friend, to the power of the tempter. Give him no advantage over you; dispute every inch of ground; instead of retreating, advance; instead of relaxing, brace anew your nerves for the conflict. Take the whole armour of God. Look upward for grace and strength to wield it. March forward to the "wicket gate," and to the glory that lies beyond. Keep your eye steadily on the Captain of your salvation. Where His banners wave, be you found, though it be in the thickest of the fight; and soon, yes soon, your trials will be over; your victory will be won; and you will have nought to do, but to lay aside your weapons, and sing the note of eternal triumph.

LETTER VII.

In my last, I recommended earnestness and sincerity, as necessary to acceptable prayer. The third particular which I mentioned was, faith in the promises.

Does not your Bible, my young friend, insist upon this? Does it not declare, that he who cometh to God, "must believe that he is, and that he is the rewarder of them that diligently seek Him?" Does it not compare to the fluctuation of the restless wave, that prayer which is offered without faith? And does it not assert, that without faith, it is impossible to please Him? But what is meant by faith in the promises, methinks I hear you say. How shall I know, when I incorporate this faith in my petition? It is not necessary, my young friend, that you know it; but it is necessary, and even indispensable, that you have it.

There is afloat, a false and vain-confident feeling, that mistakes presumption for faith. This sometimes appears in communities, which are visited by the special influences of the Holy Spirit. Ignorant and proud enthusiasts, take advantage of excited feelings, and sow the tares of error, while the servant of Jesus is scattering the seeds of truth. Some have declared, that, in praying for a blessing, we had only to believe that it would be granted, and success was certain. In praying for an individual, all we had to do was to be certain in our own minds, that the individual would be converted, and it would be so. When I look at the spirit which such people display, and find little of the meekness and humility of the gospel, I view it as presumptive evidence against their characters, and their opinions. When David prayed for the life of his child, though with deep humility and earnestness, it was not spared. When Paul thrice besought the Lord for the removal of a grievous affliction, the prayer was heard, and answered on the soul; but not as he had expected, on the body. The prayer of faith is never lost. It is invariably answered. But to assert that it will be answered in the particular way, or for the particular thing which we have expected, is both anti-scriptural and presumptuous. Here lies the error of these enthusiasts. One step farther would make them claim inspiration.

When we come to the throne of grace, we come, not to dictate, but to supplicate. God, in his word, has given us a warrant to pray for all spiritual, and many temporal favors. In praying for the former, we may, and must, be importunate and persevering until death. In respect to the latter, we must be submissive; and ever add, if it will be for thy glory, and the interests of my soul. When you pray, therefore, for spiritual blessings, you know that your prayer is according to the will of God. If it be sincere, and presented with an exclusive reference to the mediation of Christ, it will, it must be answered. I do not say, that the very things you ask, and in the precise way and time in which you look for them, will be received. Not at all. But still I say your prayer will be answered. We are short-sighted creatures. We often suppose that we know what is best for us, and would have, in our own hands, the management of our spiritual and temporal affairs. But, recollect the "ring." It is not for us to keep it. It is in the hands of God. There only, is it safe. There, no foe can reach it, and no fears need be entertained of its security.

Recollect, then, that it is yours to believe. It is God's to plan and to execute. Confidence in God's truth, and wisdom, and goodness, is the main ingredient in this prayer of faith. Say in the fullness of your confidence, I plead for this thing, O God. Although it may not be given by Thee in a manner, and at a time, which I expect, still I plead thy promise; and I know Thou art faithful to hear and answer prayer.

Permit me to refer again to my own experience, and I am not alone in this experience. Knowing that I was in a backslidden state, and feeling that for months there had been a melancholy distance between God and my soul, I gave myself to prayer. I entreated God to reclaim me, to give me repentance, and a more entire consecration of soul and body to his service. I knew that these were blessings which were according to the will of God, and I knew that he had promised in his word, to answer prayer for such blessings. With the hope that I entertained of being in covenant with Him, how could I doubt that he would answer the prayer for sanctification? But I verily supposed, that it would be by a direct influence of the Spirit on the heart. I expected that, in some favoured moment, perhaps while I was then praying, God would send down a holy influence, illuminate the darkened mind, melt the hard heart, purify the base affections, and arrest and reclaim the wanderer. This he might have done. This he sometimes does in the case of others; but it was not thus he answered my prayer.

When that season of earnest supplication had passed away, and was almost forgotten, he stretched me upon a bed of affliction, and filled my mind with darkness, and my body with torturing pains. Every device was tried to relieve, but the waves and the billows rolled deeper and darker. Why is it, I was then led to inquire, that God's hand is pressed so heavily upon me? Look back, my soul, upon thy pride, thy worldly-mindedness, thy ambition, thy sensuality, thy neglect of duty. Do not these compose the cloud that envelopes thee? are they not the pains that rack thee? Hast thou not forsaken "the fountain of living waters?" Then, like the prodigal's, my eyes were filled with remorseful tears; and I said, God is answering my prayer for humility, for spirituality, for meekness, for more entire devotedness.

Happy is that soul who can say: Oh Lord, sanctify me, if it be by fire. Sanctify me, even if it be through the deep waters of affliction.

I cite this example to show, that our prayers

must be offered, and offered in confidence. But the way and the time of their being answered, it is not for us to dictate. We may take any promise in the word of God, and with the confidence of children go to Him, and say, our Father, hast thou not said thus, and dost thou not say this to me? Let me then remind thee, O thou covenant-keeping God, of these ample promises, and let me beseech thee to fulfil them all in thy servant; and in thine own way let them be verified in my complete salvation!

LETTER VIII.

It was not my intention to extend my remarks to so great a length on the nature of prayer; but I have been insensibly led along, by my anxiety to impress upon your mind the importance of the subject. By personal experience, I have, I trust, learned its value. I have been able to trace every spiritual declension to the closet. When the enemies of my soul have triumphed, I could distinctly see that my armour had not been strengthened by prayer. When the sweet serenity of conscious forgiveness, a calm sense of Divine favor has departed, and the restless tumult of passion has succeeded, the sweet spirit, I knew full well, had not, with fervency, been wooed to my bosom.

As well might we expect vegetation to spring from the earth without the sunshine or the dew, as the Christian to unfold his graces, and advance in his course, without patient, persevering, and ardent prayer. The throne of grace must be your home, your dearest, happiest home. If unavoidably detained from your accustomed visits to the sweet retreat, O, may you feel, like the dove that fluttered anxiously around the ark, that, on earth, there is nought that is stable, on which to rest your weary foot. And, when you again find the consecrated spot, may your tears of joy, mingle with those of penitence, as you throw yourself anew into the arms of your Father and your Friend.

In my last, I spoke of praying with faith in the promises; so that I have now glanced at the three important particulars, necessary in acceptable prayer.

The second inquiry, for what you should pray, needs, it appears to me, but little consideration, if you have been taught of the Spirit. The Apostle says, "we know not what we should pray for as we ought," but "the Spirit helpeth our infirmities." It would not, therefore, become me, to enumerate the particulars which should form the subject matter of your prayers. If the Holy Spirit has wrought in your soul a deep conviction of your depravity, you will wrestle with God for its removal. "Create in me a clean heart, O God, and renew a right spirit within me." If you are suddenly betrayed into sin, and your conscience feels the heavy load, you will exclaim, "O Lord, pardon mine iniquity, for it is great." If your heart be sluggish in duty, you will, of course, and from necessity, pray, "quicken me, O Lord, and I will run in the ways of thy commandments." If you love the kingdom of Christ, you will pray earnestly, and with faith, for its coming. If you feel for the perishing condition of sinners, you will commend them, with tears, to the mercy of your God.

But your prayers will not be thus general. If you ever, as I trust you will, become a noble and devoted Christian; if you mean to put your feet in the warm tracks of a Newell or a Huntington, your prayers will often be protracted and particular. You will pray for blessings on your own soul, on your parents, on your sisters, on your neighbourhood, on the world. Your ardent mind, steeped in benevolence, will hold a familiar and holy intercourse with your Father in heaven. Not an anxiety will you feel, but you will communicate it; not a reasonable wish will you indulge, but you will express it; not a known duty wil you discover, but you will pray for grace to perform it. To enter into further particulars, would be unnecessary.

But I have one remark, before I dismiss this subject. It is this. Let nothing, if possible, hinder you, in the performance of your regular devotions, from occupying your allotted season of prayer. When the love of God is on the wane, and that of the world is waxing stronger, a trifling excuse will satisfy the conscience for the neglect of this all-important duty. May such never be your case. Such a state is filled with danger, and often a warning to a melancholy and disgraceful fall. The soul that is bent on duty, and to whom prayer is a delightful privilege, will seldom be hindred from its performance. No trifling excuse will be heeded; and if necessity for a time bar up the sacred enclosure, the heart will sicken at the void, which is created by a temporary absence from the hallowed spot. When that necessity can be removed, how will the soul leap forward to its dearest earthly home! It will seem doubly sweet, for the temporary hindrance. The soul will say, as it lays itself beneath the altar, O, blessed privilege! How long does it appear since I last enjoyed thee! How delightful to lay my head on this dear support, and feel that I am again alone with my Redeemer and my friend!

Such will be the language of the saint, when debarred for a time from the throne of grace.

Situated as you now are, you are in a measure free from the fear of such interruptions. But you will soon be ushered into new surroundings. You will soon find yourself surrounded by companions, to whom you must pay the ordinary courtesies of life. Then will you need this advice; nay, you will need the supporting hand of God, to keep you from dishonouring your profession, and forgetting the solemn vows you have recorded. Then if you persevere in the course which I have marked out, it will be evident that I have not written in vain, and that what I have written, has been attended with more than human ability.

Little do you know, as yet, of your own heart; little do you realize the seducing influence of the world, and the artful insinuations of Satan. But if you will cling to the counsel I have given, and commit your soul to the keeping of your Redeemer, those temptations you shall meet, immoveable as the rock that beats back the angry billow—you shall walk unhurt amid the flames—you shall be covered with armor—you shall weather out the storm in safety—and at last, when your temptations and trials are over, you shall sing, eternally sing, unto Him who hath loved me, and washed me from my sins, in His own blood; to him "be glory and dominion for ever and ever."

LETTER XI.

You will recollect, my young friend, that I proposed to direct you to the attainment of an elevated standard of piety. In the course of my remarks, you must ever bear in mind, I am suggesting only the important means and methods of such attainment. Ever recollect, that without the Spirit's influence, the Christian can no more advance in holiness, than the sinner repent and believe; and yet the former will be guilty for not advancing, and the latter for not complying with the demands of the gospel.

The three grand helps towards the point at which you aim, are prayer, self-examination, and a close and diligent searching of the Scriptures. The first topic has been already discussed. Imperfectly as it has been set forth, I trust you are deeply convinced of its importance; and I shall, therefore, briefly attend to the second; viz. self-examination.

This is a duty, as difficult as it is important. Every Christian acknowledges it to be so. The object of self-examination is, to obtain a correct knowledge of our moral character. Before conversion, man is generally a stranger to himself. As he comes forth from the nursery, he enters upon the reckless career of boyhood. His eye and ear are all attention, as one object after another crowds upon his view. He is full of questions concerning the remarkable views, both of art and of nature. He courts every trifle; and when obtained, throws it away in pursuit of another. But he watches not the operations of his own mind. He is, indeed, all attention to the busy world without; but, all inattention to the busy world within. And such will he continue to be, when boyhood shall give place to maturity; unless the Holy Spirit turns his eye inward on the soul. A philosopher, he may range through nature, and collect and classify her productions, and yet never sit one solitary hour in severe judgment on himself. Such a man is, in one sense, a wise man, but in another a fool. That he is a man of knowledge, no one acquainted with his attainments, can deny; but, in my opinion, he is far from being a man of wisdom, in the highest and noblest use of that term.

"Knowledge and wisdom, far from being one,
Have oft times no connexion. Knowledge dwells
In heads replete with thoughts of other men;
Wisdom in minds attentive to their own.
Knowledge is proud that he has learned so much,
Wisdom is humble that he knows no more.

It is surprising, how few persons are in the habit of attending to the operations of their own minds. The generality of mankind are so absorbed in the various pursuits of life, that no opportunity is allowed for serious self-examination. They live in a whirlpool of cares; and to them, the deeper and more boisterous the vortex, the better. They are all hurry and bustle; business and pleasure swallow up every thought; and thus life's important hours, like successive couriers, chase each other into eternity. Hence you will often find these gay dreamers, when brought to a death-bed, taking, for the first time, a direct and dreadful look at themselves. Life has been wasted away, and eternity now stares them into a consciousness of their ruin.

The Christian who is taught of the Spirit, is the only man who can be said to be acquainted with himself. Not that he can notice every hue of moral feeling; nor can he comprehend the "mystery of iniquity" that pervades the heart: for it is "deceitful above all things; who can know it?" But he is so much in the habit of noticing his moral exercises; he so frequently communes with his own heart, that he comes at length to an acquaintance with himself; and can pronounce, with humble confidence, on his present state, and his future destiny. Such a character is venerable and immoveable. Changes may occur; prosperity or adversity may come: but he walks in too high a region, to be unduly elated by the former, or sinfully depressed by the latter. What a calm, delightful, enviable summit. It is like the mountain covered with vegetation, upon whose top rest the mild beams of glory whilst, in the figurative language of Goldsmith, the "midway storm" thunders and rages beneath.

We are expressly enjoined, by the apostle, to "examine ourselves"—to "know our own selves;" for by so doing, we come to the knowledge of our true characters. If we are Christians, we may, and we must endeavour, to know it. Such knowledge will remove our fears, and add greatly to our comfort. Some, I am well aware, walk in darkness and in doubt, to the end of their journey. They see no light, until Heaven's glory breaks in upon the soul. Such, no doubt, was the case of the amiable and pious Cowper; but his case was a peculiar one.

In general, the knowledge of his personal salvation is attainable by the Christian. None should think of resting, until such assurance is attained. It may not be the will of God to give it, but it is his will that we should strive for it. If you aim at an elevated standard of piety, this will be your mark.

some persons are satisfied with just enough of religion, to ease the conscience and give encouragement for a feeble hope. They never rise above this grade, nor ever manifest more than a sort of negative character. Self-examination, they utterly neglect; or, if they pretend to practise it, they perform the duty so seldom and superficially, as to depress, rather than elevate, their own low and dimunitive standard.

Be thou not of their number. Employ every means to become thoroughly acquainted with your true character. Make religion your grand business. Let the soul be the all-absorbing subject of interest. How dreadful would it be, to pass into eternity with false hopes and mistaken views! Determine to know the worst, as well as the best of your case. Come to a personal investigation, with the spirit of an inflexible inquisitor. Go into the secret chambers of the soul, and carry thither the touchstone of salvation, the torch of truth.

In my next, I hope to enter a little more minutely into this subject. In the mean time, I commend you to the grace of Him, who is able to build you up—to enable you to go from strength to strength—to fire your flagging zeal—rouse the animating hope—and put within you the spirit of a self-denied, all-devoted Christian.

LETTER XII.

The duty of self-examination, like that of prayer, is both stated and occasional. The conscientious Christian, should not suffer a single day to pass, without an investigation of his moral character. At the close of the day, and when about to commit the keeping of his soul to Him "who never slumbereth nor sleepeth," he should take a deliberate and serious retrospect of the past. His conduct, and the motives which prompted it, should pass under investigation.

I cannot, my young friend, too strongly recommend to you this practice. The most eminent saints have been distinguished for it; and I must press upon you a similar course, if you would aim at an elevated standard of piety.

There is less difficulty attending this daily investigation, than many professors imagine. Were long intervals to occur between the periods of self-examination, we should, indeed, experience much inconvenience and perplexity in performing the duty. We should then resemble the unskillful and heedless merchant, who, yielding to habitual negligence and hurry, defers posting his books, until he is overwhelmed with their complex magnitude. But let the duty be daily and thoroughly performed, and we rise to the standard of the skillful and prudent merchant, who duly records every item of business; who never closes his counting-house, until his balance-sheet is made up; and who, by a single reference, can tell the true state of his accounts, and form a correct estimate of his commercial standing.

You will find yourself aided in this work, by a secret journal or diary, which must be excluded from the inspection of all, but God and yourself.

If you are in the habit of thus daily inquiring into your motives and conduct, you will find it an excellent preparation for approaching a throne of grace. You will perceive so many failures in duty, and such frequent commission of sin, that your soul must necessarily be humbled before God. You will also perceive whether you make any advances in knowledge and holiness, and thus discover a source of encouragement, or a stimulus to greater diligence. Your conscience will be rendered tender and faithful; and you will thus be on the alert, that you be not tempted, or drawn aside from your duty. You will walk softly amid the thorny path, nor feel the bleeding wounds which are inflicted on so many careless and worldly-minded professors.

Besides this daily process which I am recommending, there is one special season of self-examination, which you should by no means omit. The Apostle enjoins on every Christian, to examine himself before he partakes of the Lord's Supper. "Let a man examine himself, and so let him eat of that bread, and drink of that cup." This is indispensable, to a profitable attendance on this interesting and significant ordinance. If you are in the habit of daily self-examination, you will find the observance of this special season, by no means difficult or laborious. You will have acquired, by your daily self-examination, so much self-knowledge; such a tact, if I may be allowed the expression, at seizing upon evidence, and analyzing feelings and motives, that, instead of proving an unwelcome task, it will constitute a satisfactory, comforting, and delightful duty.

The reason why so many complain of the difficulty of a proper discharge of this duty, is obvious. I shall, in a subsequent letter, disclose it more fully.

Be assured, my young friend, that, if ever you arrive at an elevated standard of piety, you will attribute it, as much to a strict and persevering self-examination, as to any other means, which it is, under God, your privilege to use. It is through a neglect of this, that Christianity makes, in most of us, such a stunted appearance. It is for the want of this, that hypocrisy vaunts itself in the attire of piety. It is for the want of this, that doubts, and fears, and disquietude, and backslidings, are so prevalent. I entreat you, therefore, as you value your peace and your improvement, to persevere in the faithful discharge of this duty. You will be abundantly rewarded. Faith will walk arm in arm with the promises; hope, instead of a flickering light, will become a steady radiation from an unclouded sun; love will grow to a flame, that "many waters cannot quench;" and zeal, founded in truth, and directed by knowledge, will hold on, until death, its vigorous and untiring career.

I say not, that you will at once arrive at this lofty elevation. Ah, now, you may have many a thorny path to tread, many a rugged way to traverse, many a difficult hill to climb. Nights of weeping, and days of darkness and of tempest may intervene. But God will interpose in your behalf; he will "temper the wind to the shorn lamb."

Recollect, for your encouragement, that the farther you proceed, the easier and the more delightful will be the passage. As it approximates heaven, it partakes of celestial beauty. Like the fine, free avenue to a noble metropolis, the proximity of this road to the heavenly Jerusalem, opens wider, and shows clearer, and almost admits the eager eye to catch the spires of glory, as they glitter in the light of heaven. Take up your cross, dear youth, and march forward. While you may encounter difficulties, you may also partake of many pleasures; pleasures which are as much superior to the sickly joys of earth, as the river of life is purer, than the green waters of an offensive and stagnant pool.

"The hill of Zion yields
A thousand sacred sweets;
Before we reach the heavenly fields,
Or walk the golden streets."

To me, it has ever appeared strange, that when so much depends on the duty of self-examination, it should be so generally neglected.

We do not thus act in our temporal sins. If the claim to an estate be attended with any degree of doubt or embarrassment, we spare no pains to give it a thorough investigation. If the body be disordered, we are alive to every symptom, and we watch every new aspect of the disease. But in respect to the soul, we are at little pains to substantiate its hope, by actual examination. We live along, as if the matter were settled; as if we had a guarantee for our heavenly inheritance: when, in fact, all is doubt and embarrassment; when, perhaps, we may have only "a name to live, whilst we are dead."

Let this duty, my young friend, be viewed by you as altogether indispensable. Set about it with diligence. Should your enemy, knowing its usefulness and importance, attempt to discourage you, listen not to the voice of the tempter. Renew your labour; call upon God to fix your thoughts, and to give you success. Persevere, even unto death, in a duty so necessary to your safety, and essential to your comfort.

LETTER XIII.

It was suggested, in my last, that I should pursue my remarks a little farther, upon self-examination. My reasons for so doing, are, the importance of the subject, and the general neglect of it with which many Christians are chargeable.

Since the duty is so intimately connected with your hope of salvation, your advancement in holiness, and your general elevation of character; you will bear with me a little longer, even though the subject should appear to be destitute of those incidental attractions, which are peculiar to the ordinary accomplishments of life. You must first lay the solid column; the Corinthian capital may then be added on, My conscience would condemn me, were I to speak first of external conduct, when the piety of the soul is superior, and demands the first and deepest consideration. Let this be obtained, and, I doubt not, your manners and deportment will take that elevated and noble character, which will secure to you the love of the virtuous, and the respect and admiration of all.

Fixing the attention on manners and deportment, before the heart is rectified, is like profusely adorning the exterior of a building, when it is all unfinished and comfortless within. You are allured, by the imposing aspect which it presents; but upon entering, how great is your disappointment, to find, not only, no correspondence in the interior, but every thing cheerless and forbidding. It is certainly more pleasing, to view even a homely exterior, an outside that promises but little, and to perceive within, beauty, harmony, and elegance. Happy will you be, if, gifted as you are, with at least an agreeable person, you can so irradiate your mind with knowledge and holiness, as to throw around you an additional attraction, and make your soul approximate to the comeliness of an unfallen spirit. But I have left the subject and must return.

The difficulty of arriving at a knowledge of our true character, does not arise from any deficiency or obscurity in evidence, as recorded in the word of God; but from the manner of applying that evidence to ourselves. The liability to deception lies here. We cannot say, that we have the evidence, because we may have deceiving and hypocritical feelings, which our self-love may mistake for genuine Christian emotions. The word of God is full, clear, and explicit. It marks out the true disciple of Christ, with unerring exactness. The evidence is direct and and indirect, positive and negative, in example or embodied principle.

The direct evidence, is that which consists in a record of the feelings which every Christian must possess. The Bible is full of this. The indirect, is that which may be inferred, from precepts and principles. The positive, is exhibited in all those commands which relate to doing the will of God. The negative, from example or embodied principle, is that which is derived from the conduct of the patriarchal and primitive saints.

Thus you see the Bible is full of evidence relating to the character of the genuine follower of Christ. That evidence is clear and explicit, presented under various forms, and couched in the simplest terms. Where, then, lies the difficulty of correctly ascertaining, at once, our true character? I will tell you. It lies in the depravity of the human heart. That heart, as I have already observed, is "deceitful above all things;" and this is the true reason, why we cannot appropriate this evidence, with the certainty of its application.

But I will enter into a few particulars, for your farther satisfaction, to show you that self-examination is as difficult, as it is important; and that nothing but a long course of painful, persevering effort, will bring you to a confidence, unshaken by doubt, of your being a child of God, and a joint heir with Jesus Christ. You do not wish to have a name to live, and still be dead. You do not desire to go into eternity, with a profession only. No, you wish not to be deceived in so momentous an affair; for the world, you would not be deceived. You have counted the cost; you have surveyed the cross; and you are determined to follow your Lord. You will not then be discouraged, when I inform you, that to deal with your own heart, in close examination, is a great and difficult work. But the difficulty, as I before observed, will diminish with diligence.

One great reason why so little satisfaction is obtained in the work, is, that our investigation is not complete. We do not come to it with a determination to be thorough in its performance. Although we acknowledge that there is no duty so difficult, nor any more important; yet there is none, perhaps, more superficially performed. Although our hopes, our peace of mind, our growth in grace, are intimately connected with close self-examination; yet, how easily are we discouraged by obstacles which the enemies of our souls may interpose; and how hastily do we run through the duty, deriving no satisfaction, but only enveloping the mind in still deeper gloom. After one or two such superficial trials, some will give up the duty as impractical, and live along in doubt, and die, perhaps, in distressing uncertainty.

We are less thorough in this spiritual investigation, than we should be in almost any other subject. No wonder, then, that we make such slow advances in self-knowledge; no wonder, that it is generally viewed as impractical, when so superficially performed. When you, my young friend, enter upon this duty, make, I entreat you, sure work with your soul; explore the secret motives, and analyze the fleeting feelings. If it cost years of persevering labour, ascertain, if possible, whether you have an inheritance on high. May God, by his Spirit, assist you, and make you successful.

LETTER XIV.

I OBSERVED, in my last, that we were in danger of being superficial in the work of self-examination. There will be a strong temptation to this, from our natural indolence, as well as the difficulties to be overcome. Hence, you will find few Christians, who make this duty a serious and indispensable business. A little hasty catechising, just before they celebrate the Lord's Supper, is all that is deemed necessary. Two or three months may intervene, during which, the soul, and its momentous affairs, are comparatively neglected. When again summoned to renew their vows, over the melting memorials of a Saviour's love, they begin to think of some preparation; but one moment steals upon the heels of another, and the business is deferred, until the hour when the inviting bell is calling them to the feast. Then, all is agitation and hurry, when all should be calm, collected, and contemplative. They leave to themselves, perhaps, a few moments, to relieve the sould from a tumult of cares; and after an ineffectual and superficial attempt at self-examination, they go trembling in doubt, or fearlessly in cold-hearted presumption.

Such is the character of many who profess to be aiming at the crown of glory. They do not sit in judgment on the internal man, as did David, when he threw open the chambers of his secret soul, and exclaimed, "Search me, O God, and know my heart; try me, and know my thoughts; and see if there be any wicked way in me, and lead me in the way everlasting." It is mere half-way work with them. Conscience prejudges and condemns. To silence her clamours, it is necessary that they make, at least, a show of self-examination. But when they take up the sacred record, they find so little there, which can be honestly appropriated in their favour, that they are obliged, if they would glean any thing for their encouragement, to misinterpret and misapply its meaning. When they meet with such a sweeping declaration as this, "If any man love the world, and the things that are in the world, the love of the Father is not in him;" when their eyes glance at so discriminating a text, they employ a flase reasoning, to midify its severity, or avert its applications.

There is, recollect, a strong temptation to be

partial in this important work. Self-love, prompts us to look more eagerly for the favourable, than the unfavourable evidence; and gives us a greater readiness in applying the former than the latter. It is an object with our spiritual enemies, to flatter us into a belief of our good estate, that we may omit our watch, and indulge our vain-confident expectations. Thousands are, by this means, led blind-folded down to ruin.

The superficial Christian, seizes the most uncertain evidence. It will not take much to persuade him that all is safe. If a vast amount of Scripture is against him, and he can yet find but here and there a single text, whose aspect in his case, is, to say the least, doubtful, how eagerly will he grasp it, and cast it into the favourable scale. It is, with him, a principle, to be in his favour, neutralize a hundred others, which are most certain against him. Hence you will sometimes hear professing Christians declare, that were it not for this one text, "We know that we have passed from death unto life, because we love the brethren;" they should be driven to despair.

This may, indeed, be the language of a sincere disciple; of one who walks in darkness, but who goes mourning over his personal deficiency. Far be it from me, to discourage such. This precious text was recorded by the compassionate Spirit, for him; and often, when the billows were high, and the prospect all darkness, it has beamed like a star of hope upon his trembling soul, and saved it from despair and death. But, when I hear it quoted by a thoughtless, worldly-minded professor, I account it a sad mark against him. Is this the only text, to which he can cling? Let him recollect, that the same apostle also said, "By this we know that we love the children of God, when we love God, and keep his commandments."

The superficial professor, seems determined, if possible, to make the Bible speak in his favour. He comes not to that infallible touchstone, with a sincere desire to probe his heart, to examine the reason of his hope, and to scrutinize the foundation of his confidence. He comes not, with a resolution to make thorough and impartial work; but to make the word of God, like the fabled oracles of heathenism, speak a language unclear and uncertain.

Now, my young friend, be thou of a different spirit. Go into this investigation, with a resolution that you will be thorough and impartial.

Say to your Bible, I will consult thee faithfully, thou infallible Book. I will let thy light into the darkest chambers of my heart. The sword of the Spirit shall search the system, and probe my wounded nature, in the tenderest part. I will not shirnk from the inquiry, but will enter upon it sincerely, and perservere in it through life.

LETTER XV.

The character of the superficial professor, I must carry along with me, in order to show you the importance and the happiness of aiming at a high standard of attainment.

He is a miserable self-deceiver, who imagines that any advantage is gained, by persuading himself, contrary to evidence, that he is a Christian. And yet there are thousands of this character. Why do they not reflect on God's omniscience? Why do they not consider, that their own good opinion of themselves, will not alter their true character. God looketh upon the heart. He strips the outward man, and carries his judicial sentence home upon the soul. He can tear from the heart its most artful disguises, and look with an eye of infallible decision on its emotions. With his "fan in his hand," he will pass through the visible church, "and gather his wheat into the garner; but he will burn up the chaff with unquenchable fire."

He who attends to self-examination superficially, places too much confidence in the judgment of others. Every person knows, that if another's opinion be coincident with our own, we are flattered by it. This is especially the case, when it respects our religious character. Some, who are fearful of deception, will, I am well aware, never admit the opinion of others to have any weight. This is, certainly, the safest extreme. Such are, generally, mourning Christians, who are much more prone to form an unfavourable, than a flattering opinion, of their condition. But others are disposed to place undue reliance on the judgment of those who have expressed the belief that they are Christians. This satisfies them; especially if it be the judgment of those, whom they greatly respect, and whose discernment as to moral character, they have been in the habit of considering as well nigh infallible. Perhaps it is merely the wish of a beloved friend, or the expression of parental hope, rather than a deliberate and formal decision, upon ascertained evidence; still it is, often enough to undermine the duty of close self-examination, and induce a carelessness, and a confidence, awfully prophetic of deep delinquency, and melancholy backsliding.

It will be evident to you, my young friend, that confidence, if it have no better foundation, is nothing less than presumption; and that it may, ere long, lead to great doubt and perplexity, if not to absolute despair.

The hope of eternal life, is not to be taken up on slight grounds. It is a subject to be settled between God and your own soul. I would not despise the advice, nor reject, entirely, the opinion of others; but I would be careful, not to trust too much to such advice and opinion. Since you are to stand or fall by the word of God, it is to that, and to that alone, you must look for testimony in your case. The advice and the opinion of ministers, and private Christians, you will seek and respect; but you will not regard them as infallible, nor place your reliance upon them. Let them neither sink you to despair, nor elevate you to a vain confidence.

You know full well, that no finite being can pronounce with certainty on your spiritual condition. Even the holy apostles, who were under the immediate inspiration of God, were not endued with this prerogative. Were they not deceived respecting the characters of Simon Magus, of Demas, and of others? How, then, can we trust our souls to the opinion of fallible man? What reliance can we place on anything, short of God, and His unerring oracles?

I dwell the longer on this topic, because I have not seen the point brought out fully, in any of the experimental treatises which have fallen under my observation; and because there is in most persons, a strong tendency to lean upon the judgment of others, rather than to be at the pains of a severe and strict investigation for themselves. You cannot be ignorant, that such a course must be unsafe, and unsatisfactory. How much better, to go at once to the Bible? If we there find our character to be that of the saints who have gone before us, what joy and assurance will it give! We know that we are standing on a rock—we feel that it is stable as eternity. But, if we lean to human opinion, we shall ever find our evidences equivocal, and our hope neither sure nor steadfast.

Remember, too, my young friend, that those who love us, and who wish us to become Christians, are very liable to be satisfied with the shadow of evidence. They grasp at the first hopeful appearances, and pronounce often a favourable decision, when there are not sufficient grounds to warrant it. When you recollect this, you will receive their opinion with the greater hesitancy, and feel more deeply, the importance of settling the question over your Bible; between God and your own soul. Man can look only at the outside; his limited vision cannot penetrate within. But God looketh on the heart; on that wandering, wayward heart, the seat of so many joys and sorrows, the abode of so much deceitfulness and impurity. He knows its character. He analyzes its emotions.

To him, therefore, carry your soul, and, with David, invoke his scrutiny. Then will you be able to give to him that asketh you, "a reason of the hope that is you, with meekness and fear." Then you shall have "the peace of God which passeth all understanding." Your title to a heavenly inheritance, shall bear the royal signet; a seal which none on earth dare question; and which, when the gates of death shall be unbarred, shall give you free access to the royal presence, and to the temple of God on high. Rest satisfied with nothing short of this seal—and may the Lord enable you to persevere in seeking it.

LETTER XVI.

IN prosecuting the work of self-examination, there is another danger to which you will be liable, and against which I would guard you—a reliance upon past experience. If you suffer this to have a practical influence upon you, it will paralyze every effort, and make you to sit down in indolence, satisfied with present attainments, when you should be pressing towards the mark, for the prize of your high calling.

I mention this, because it is a very common fault, and one but little regarded. What can be pleaded in defense of such spiritual sluggishness, I cannot conceive.

The holy Apostle, who, next to his Lord, is the brightest example which is set before us, counted all his past attainments as nothing, so long as any interval remained between him, and the perfection which is in Christ Jesus. Hence he compares himself to one struggling in a race, reaching forth, and pressing towards the prize which was set before him. What a beautiful figure—reaching forth, pressing towards—mark the expressions.

If you had ever seen an Olympic race, where there were numerous competitors; if you had ever witnessed their earnestness, as they approached the goal—every muscle strained to the utmost, and the hand reaching forward to seize the crown—you would have a more impressive idea of this beautiful comparison. May you, by happy experience, know its import. But, my young friend, I must confess, that there are few, very few, of these Olympic strugglers, in the Christian race. Too many are satisfied to look on as spectators, while a few only, run and win the prize. Too many loiter in the course, or turn off into the by-paths of iniquity. They base their confidence on past experience. They seem to have settled the point once for all. They will perhaps admit, that, as to present evidence of Christian character, they have not much to offer; but they refer you to the time when their evidence was clear and certain. "There was a period," say they, "when we experienced conversion. A great change took place in our feelings, affections, and conduct. We can no more doubt that it was the work of God, than that our bodies are a part of His creation. Others saw and acknowledged the change. 'Tis true, we do not feel now, as we did then; but we were told that this abatement of feeling, was to be expected; that the ardour of the youthful convert could not last forever." Ask such vain-confident persons, for the evidence of their faith, and they refer you immediately to this previous hope. They are at no pains to inquire for the present evidences of their being in a state of salvation. The business was settled years ago. Others, who will not go quite to this length, will secretly feed their hopes too much upon the past, instead of inquiring into present marks of grace. It is a sad proof, that they are either deceived with false appearances, or declining from God, and from duty.

I do not mean, by these remarks, to imply, that we are never to recur to past experience, for hope and consolation. I believe we are permitted, by the word of God, and the examples of his saints, so to do. David, in a time of deep trouble, said, "I will remember thee, from the land of Jordan, from the Hermonites, and from the hill Mizar."

But what I wish to guard you against, my young friend, is placing too much confidence in the past and suffering it to operate as an opiate to present vigilance and activity. Past experience is one of the devil's lures to vain confidence; one of the main schemes of hypocrisy; one of the most common and fatal grounds of self-deception. Even Paul, would not trust to the past, although he had been struck blind by a beatific vision of his Master, and introduced into His kingdom, under circumstances so striking and peculiar. No, forgetting all that is past, "he presses towards the mark for the prize of his high calling in Christ Jesus."

These old hopes, this former experience, you cannot depend upon. As well might you think of crossing the ocean in a worm-eaten vessel. While the weather was mild, and the sea calm, you might float in apparent security; but should the heavens grow dark, and the billows begin to beat upon the vessel, you would fall a speedy prey to the all-devouring wave. The Christian, who has no better basis than by-gone experience to rest upon, may live on, amid the sunshine of life, in apparent ease and comfort; but in that hour when God taketh away the soul, he will long for something more substantial to cling to, than a doubtful and previous hope.

Many are thus fatally deceived. To them, life seems to glide onward undisturbed, and the soul is rocked asleep on the pillow of past experience. Conscience may be so far stupefied, as not even to arouse at the call of death. They may knock at heaven's gate, but they may also hear the dread voice within, "I know you not, depart from me, ye workers of iniquity."

Such self-deceivers will not acknowledge the duty of daily self-examination. It is impossible to rouse them to the performance of it. They are cased in an impenetrable armor. They have, in this past experience, an antidote to every fear, and an apology for every delinquency. O, be thou not of their number. Look for daily evidence of salvation. It is present evidences that are called for, and such cannot be given, without a daily, habitual, self-examination. In all your past experience, there is, to say the least, a possibility of your having been deceived; it is therefore not a sufficient ground of trust. You must be ready now, "to give to him that asketh, the reason of the hope that is within you." If you pursue the course which I have marked out, you shall never need to bring forward an old and antedated hope, as the only evidence of your faith; but in every look, and word, and action, you shall make it certain to all, that you are in deed and in truth, a Christian.

LETTER XVII.

Assurance of salvation, or even a well-grounded, uniform, and scriptural hope, is a blessing which is not attained by a superficial and infrequent self-examination. It is not generally enjoyed until after a series of persevering, and well applied exertions. Sometimes, where there *is* a desire to be thorough and diligent, it is not enjoyed. It appears to be the will of God, that some should go weeping after it, even to the grave. But generally, if Christians are faithful, they will arrive at a confirmed and satisfactory hope of eternal life.

There is difficulty, I admit, in the work of self-examination. "Even the righteous are scarcely saved—saved in many instances as by fire." The heart is so deceitful, and the enemies of our soul so full of evil scheming, that we are liable to draw too favourable conclusions of our being in a state of salvation. There are times too, when we seem afraid to uncover our bosoms to the piercing glance of God. Like merchants who are on the borders of bankruptcy, we shrink from making a thorough investigation of our accounts. We tremble at the thought of finding ourselves spiritual bankrupts, and are almost willing, if I may be allowed the comparison, to forge evidences in our favour, and to our own deception.

This is especially the character of one who is not habitually and daily engaged in the work of self-examination. There is an uncertainty and confusion about his hopes, which make him afraid to enter too deeply into the state of his circumstances. He does not open the Bible, and appeal to its searching truths. He fears that the scrutiny would sweep down his cherished expectations. He is, therefore, tempted to hunt out only those portions of scripture, which appear to favour his case; and to blind his vision to those, which would shake his confidence, or eradicate his hopes. When he would examine himself respecting the love or the renunciation of sin, he is far from being a thorough and impartial censor. He can yield up some of the least-loved sinful habits, and can give full credit to himself for the self-denial; but the "right hand" and the "right eye" are not parted with. Some worldly project is in view, which opposes too severe a standard of religious character;

and which would be found to be inconsistent, by too close an application to Bible ethics. Accordingly, instead of making the world yield to the claims of Christianity, he must narrow down Christianity to accommodate the world.

Business, pleasure, and reputation, when they get the mastery, make self-examination an irksome and unpleasant duty. When a Christian professor is too eager in pursuit of them, he always feels a conviction of delinquency, depriving him of that free and noble air, which is ever the concomitant of an approving conscience; and filling his mind with feeble apologies for himself, or with unjust censures against his superiors in piety.

Now, can such a person come fearlessly up to the work of self-examination? Can he take the Bible in his hand, and appeal to the heart-searching God? Can he be a faithful inquisitor of the internal man? Will he not gloss over his sin? Will he not hunt for evidence to neutralize his guilt?

Such a character is satisfied with just enough of religion to make him respectable here, and afford a vague hope of happiness hereafter. But, alas! he is disappointed in both. He is viewed as hypocritical and insincere, by many of his fellow men: and there is great reason to apprehend, that, when God cometh to "make up his jewels," he will be found, not among them, but with unbelievers in the regions of despair.

It is by exhibiting to your view, my young friend, this superficial and flimsy Christianity, that I would warn you against it, and rouse you to diligence in aiming at an elevated standard of piety. Whilst there are difficulties connected with the performance of Christian duties, difficulties of no common magnitude, they are still not insurmountable. The timid and the hesitating shrink and despond; but the true child of God knows that he has enlisted in a warfare that cannot end but with life. When he puts his hand to God's covenant, when he gives his name to the Captain of his salvation, it is a deliberate and well-considered act. He has counted the cost. He has surveyed the enemy; and whilst he acknowledges his own feebleness, he confides in that pledged assistance and protection, which will render him unconquerable.

I hope that you have thus considered the subject, and determined to make a thorough and well-disciplined disciple. I trust, that with you, religion shall be all in all. It must be the business of every day; it must be the business of life.

It is a grand mistake, to suppose that the superficial Christian can possess spiritual enjoyments. They are not for him. They are for the laborious, the self-denied, the pains-taking Christian. It is the soldier who sleeps in his armour; springs to his post at a word; rushes into the thickest of the fight; and deals his well-directed blows upon the enemy: it is he, and he alone, upon whom his admiring commander bestows the meed of honour, and the trophies of victory.

Be it yours to imitate him in the spiritual conflict, and it shall be yours to share, like him, in the rewards of conquest: and even far before him shall you be honoured, for you shall sit at the King's table, and partake of the rich provisions of his temple. Every thing urges you to diligence and to duty; your honour and your happiness; your safety and your reward. O then, forgetting the things which are behind, reach forth; press onward; and the prize, the glorious prize, shall be soon and forever yours.

LETTER XVIII.

SELF-EXAMINATION, respects both feeling and conduct. A difficulty occurs in ascertaining whether the former is according to the spirit, and the latter correspondent with the precepts of the Bible. I am persuaded that you are already impressed with the importance of the duty, and are resolved that it shall occupy a prominent place in the daily exercises of the closet.

But methinks I hear you inquire, in what way you are to proceed; how you are to know that you pursue the duty to advantage; and whether you are not, after all, liable to deception? I have already forewarned you of difficulties which will appear very difficult, and which, at the very threshold of your Christian course, will be thrown in your way, to arrest your progress, and frighten you from the discharge of duty. But, be not discouraged nor intimidated. Repeated efforts in prayer to God, will enable you to face the opposition; and that which at first appeared to abound with difficulties, will be found, after a few minor discouragements, easy and delightful.

Satan will exert his utmost power to hinder

you from this all-important duty. He knows how much your hopes, and your advancement in holiness, depend upon the faithful discharge of it. Having, in so many other cases, succeeded in hindering its performance, he will hope in yours to succeed. May the grace of God enable you to disappoint him. May you persevere, even amid discouragements, until the duty shall become to you a most precious privilege.

When you enter upon this work, you will first look upward to heaven, in a few short petitions, that God would grant you his holy spirit; that he would fix your attention on the immediate duty before you; that He would keep you from a superficial investigation; and enable you to deal closely and thoroughly with your heart.

We are very liable, in our retirement, to wandering thoughts; and I doubt not, that hours have been wasted in the closet, in a vain attempt to fix the mind, while it evaded the effort, and sported itself in a fanciful and foolish visions.

It is important, therefore, that we at once counteract this unsettled state of mind, by fervent prayer to God. We should then, in a measure, anticipate Satan, who is always most busy with the children of God, when they are the nearest to duty, and are about to receive some great spiritual benefit.

Our self-examination, I have already said, respects our state of feelings, and our external conduct. Has the former partaken of the spirit of Christ? Has the latter corresponded with his precepts? It is no very difficult matter for a conscientious and reflecting individual to retrace the occurrences of a single day. But, if the business be deferred for weeks and months, his sins will be multiplied and forgotten, amid the fluctuating scenes of life. Conscious that there has been much, in both heart and life, to condemn, but forgetting the particulars, he is obliged to repent in the gross.

But he who daily calls himself to an account, will, after a few trials, find the employment both easy and edifying. With what feelings, he will ask, did I awake? Did my gratitude for nocturnal repose and protection, rise with the rising light, to Him, who is the watchman of Israel, and who never slumbereth nor sleepeth? Or was I, like the brute, indifferent to the kindness of my heavenly Guardian? Did I arise with the breath of praise on my lips, and the spirit of devotion in my heart? Or were my thoughts scattered and unsettled? In my morning devotions, can I say that I enjoyed a near access to God, so that I communed with him, even as it were, from the mercy-seat? Did I wrestle? Did I agonize? Was this the spirit, or were my prayers formal and forced? Was my frame of mind sluggish and cold? Were my petitions hurried and insincere? Did I really desire the blessings I sought; or did I only mention them as a necessary part of prayer? Had I a deep sense of my unworthiness, and a full conviction of the necessity of my Mediator's blood and merits? In my petitions, was my soul drawn forth in solicitude for others; or did I confine them to myself?

Having left my closet, did I watch unto prayer? I besought God to keep me from sin; but has my conduct, this day, been in unison with my prayers? I prayed for sanctification; but have I detected and suppressed the first risings of secret iniquity? I entreated God for more light and knowledge; but have I meditated on his works, and studied his word? I deprecated my easily besetting sin; but have I endeavoured to avoid it? I prayed for Zion, and for the salvation of the impenitent; but have I spoken a word of warning of exhortation to any person this day? Have I watched the leadings of Providence? Have I advanced in the knowledge of God? Have I made any new discoveries of his glory? Have I learned more of the scheming of Satan? or seen deeper into the deceitfulness of my own heart?

These are a few general questions, which may serve as a guide, to one who wishes an outline of daily self-examination.

LETTER XIX.

In my last communication, I instituted some inquiries, which, as I supposed, would be profitably connected with a review of the day. I am aware, my young friend, that one person cannot lay down rules on this subject, which shall apply precisely to the feelings and circumstances of others. I give you, therefore, only a sketch, by which your inexperience may possibly be benefited.

The questions which one would wish to propose, in taking a review of the day, must of course vary, according to circumstances.

I, who am a minister, and who have the care of souls, must inquire, more particularly, into my fidelity. Have I wrestled this day, for the souls of my dear people? Have I improved every opportunity to do them good? Have I preached the truth as it is in Jesus, etc.?

But you, in inquiring into your conduct, must adapt those inquiries to the circumstances by which *you* are surrounded. You have personal and relative duties, which are peculiar. Parental esteem and obedience, are obligatory. How, you should inquire, have I conducted towards my dear parents this day? Have I eased any of their cares? Have I been obedient and affectionate? I have sisters; have I done my duty towards them, instructing them, and exhibiting an example which they might with safety follow? I am surrounded by companions, some of whom profess the same hopes as myself; but others are yet in "the gall of bitterness and the bonds of iniquity;" have I, so far as opportunity would permit, encouraged the former, and warned the latter? What studies have I pursued, or what books read? What benefit have I derived from either? Have I done any thing this day for the glory of God? These are some of the questions which I should suppose would occur to one in your circumstances.

If, upon such a daily review, you find that you have advanced in holiness; that you have gained an advantage over your spiritual enemies; that you have profited by the means which a kind Providence has given for your improvement; it will afford matter for praise and thanksgiving. It will kindle up a lively gratitude in your soul, and give enjoyment to your devotions. If you discover much to condemn, many sins and failures, as you undoubtedly will, it will afford subject for humiliation, and prostrate the soul in penitential confession before God. Thus, while you advance in the knowledge of your own heart, you will have all the ingredients of acceptable worship. Your prayer will be full of praise, and full of contrition. Your mercies will call forth the one, and your transgressions prompt the other. Prayer, with you, will then be, not a cold formality, but a deep spiritual intercourse with God, and your own heart.

This dark ordeal will bring into view, and make precious, the merits and intercessions of Jesus, your High Priest and Saviour. A review, even of a single day, must, if it be close and careful, ever cover you with confusion of face. The sins committed, even in that short period, will appear numerous. The soul would sink under their heavy load, were it not for the encouraging promise: "If any man sin, we have an advocate with the Father, Jesus Christ the righteous." As sins appear numerous and aggravated, Jesus must ever appear proportionably precious. You will cast yourself all guilty in his arms, and find that "though sin has abounded, grace doth much more abound." After such a review as I have recommended, will a new application be made, and a new pardon supplicated, from the hand of the Saviour. He will thus be brought constantly in view, and made increasingly dear and delightful.

You see, then, how many and great are the advantages connected with frequent and close self-examination. Can you, then, live without it a single day? Are you not resolved that, under all ordinary circumstances, it shall be entered upon and performed with as much punctuality, as prayer and the reading of the word of God? I am persuaded, that, after what has been said, you will by no means omit it. I think you must perceive, too, that the difficulties, though great, may, by the plan which I propose, be all surmounted. They arise, as I have before observed, from neglect. Days, weeks, and months, roll away; and the soul, immersed in the busy cares of life, contracts a defilement, and collects a rubbish, which a momentary and hurried examination may render visible, but can never remove.

The soul of the delinquent is neglected—shamefully neglected. He deserves to have his hope obscured, his faith weakened, his doubts increased. He may be left amid these perplexities, until he is suddenly called to a death-bed, and compelled to take a direct look at his case. It is then a fearful scene. Clouds and darkness curtain his dying pillow; anguish insupportable heaves his wavering bosom. There is no clear sunshine upon his soul; but he lies on the fluctuating wave, uncertain whether he shall outride the beating storm.

Would you avoid such a scene? O, yes, I know you would. Then know yourself, ere it arrive. Be faithfully and intimately acquainted with your own heart. Then shall your life be happy and useful; and your death serene, perhaps gloriously triumphant. May you live the life, and die the death of the righteous!

LETTER XX.

As an important auxiliary means of advancing in holiness, I would recommend, in addition to this daily self-examination, an attention to the same duty, at stated and peculiar seasons: such, for example, as the commencement of a new year, the recurrence of your birth-day, or when about to enter upon some important change in life. By reading the biography of those saints who have been most distinguished for exalted piety, you will find that they never permitted such periods to pass by unobserved, or unimproved.

There is something in the periodical revolution of the seasons, which cannot fail to strike with seriousness a reflecting mind. A single day is of vast importance. When passed, it can never be recalled. With all its cares, its pleasures, and its pains, it has sunk into eternity. It has gone to give tidings of moral conduct, which will be faithfully recorded against the great day of account. Who, then, but the most foolish will dare to murder its hours amid feasting and mirth, when those hours are so fleeting, and so pregnant with eternal results? If a day is so important, a week, a month, or a year, proportionately increases in value; and forms a period, in which much may be done, either to grieve the spirit of God, and effect the ruin of the soul, or to promote the cause of our Redeemer, and secure to ourselves an inheritance in the kingdom of glory.

I trust you will, at least annually, review your diary. As one year rolls away, and another succeeds, look back upon the past, and forward to the future. If you have been daily in the habit of self-examination, this will be not a difficult, but an easy task, abounding with spiritual benefit. As you retrace the events of the year, the blessings which you have received will inspire you with affectionate confidence, and adoring gratitude; and the evils of heart and of life, which have marked that period, will fill your soul with penitential sorrow; and like David, prostrate in the dust of humiliation, you will be constrained to sing, both of mercy and of judgment.

What have I done, during the past year, to advance the glory of my Redeemer's kingdom? Have I done all that my means and circumstances would allow? What victories have I obtained over myself? Is my easily besetting sin laid aside, or does it too often master my strongest resolutions? Have I a deeper and more intimate communion with God, than when the year commenced? Are my desires for holiness stronger? Have I made any apparent advances towards that elevation at which I profess to aim? Are my devotions colder and more infrequent? Do my sins oftener prevail, and is the world gaining on my esteem and my attention?

These, my young friend, are some of the questions, which the observance of such a season would prompt. Let them be seriously met, and sincerely answered. Let a day, if practicable, be specially appropriated to the duty, and let it be accompanied by fasting and prayer.

The time would fail me, to enumerate all the advantages, and exhibit the full importance of such periodical investigations. Enter upon them with diligence, and prosecute them with fidelity, and you will find by your own happy experience, that self-examination is not only an important, but an easy and delightful duty.

Your experience and your careful observance of the past, will enable you to calculate for the future. Against the temptations which have proved most successful, you can place a double guard. The circumstances in which you have found yourself peculiarly exposed, you can avoid. The means which have proved most effective for your good, and the individuals whose counsels have stimulated you to duty, will be noted: and in future, the former will be oftener resorted to, and the latter drawn into more constant and intimate communion.

Your birth-day ought also to be improved. I know that many spend that day in feasting and merriment. They deem it an occasion for mirth and excitement. Herod made a royal banquet, and assembling all the wealth and beauty of the kingdom, celebrated his birth-day with music and dancing. Many with more limited means, and on a smaller scale, imitate his example. But is there any thing in our birth-day, to demand such a parade of folly? Is it a matter of mirth and rejoicing, that another year of our short lives has forever gone? Should we celebrate our own speedy career to God's judgment bar, with music and the dance? And especially, if the soul be unreconciled to God, should we chant a jubilee over its approach to hell?

If any have reason to rejoice, it is the Christian. He is one year nearer his eternal and happy home. But he views himself as so deficient, and his work on earth as so momentous, that he is far from wishing to spend his birthday in feasting. With him it should be a day of serious examination and humiliation. It should be consecrated to God, and to the prosperity of the soul.

I hope that you will observe it in this manner, and then it will be a sort of spiritual landmark, to which you can recur amid the tumultuous sea of life; and when your days are numbered on earth, you will be found to have spent them in "wisdom's ways, which are ways of pleasantness;" and you will look back upon life, though with deep humility, yet without any heart-rending regret.

LETTER XXI.

There are so many excellent works, on the preparation of the heart necessary to an acceptable approach to the Lord's Supper, that I shall do little more than to refer you to them. The only objection which I have ever felt to the use of such treatises, is, that by the numerous items which they have recommended, I have been confused, and sometimes discouraged, in the work of self-examination. If some of them were greatly abridged, and were disencumbered of a multitude of particulars, which it is impossible to carry in the memory, they would, in my opinion, be far more useful. Still, my young friend, I would habitually consult them. They are written, generally, by men of the deepest and most fervent piety, who have not taken those superficial views of church communion, which, among many denominations, are so prevalent. Where they are derived, directly, from the clear testimony of Scripture, they will save you much trouble in collating the passages, which apply more immediately to the subject in hand.

After all, the word of God is the only true standard: and to one who is familiar with the sacred volume, it will not be an irksome task to select the passages which he deems applicable to the work of self-examination. For my own part, I have ever found it attended with the greatest satisfaction, to go directly to the fountain head. Take the Bible in your hand, and ponder over it with an intention to sift your evidences of Christian character. Accompany that perusal, with fervent applications to God for light and knowledge; and you will experience a degree of satisfaction, which no other mode can afford.

Esteem the sacramental season as one of your most precious privileges. It is then that you are invited to sup at the royal banquet. You have a place at the King's table, and it becomes you to array the soul in the beauties of holiness. Were you invited to the table of some earthly monarch, how eagerly would you anticipate the honour; and what concern would you feel, that your apparel might be appropriate, and your conduct correct! But what is this honour, compared with that of sitting at the table of your Lord? See then that you are adorned with the wedding garment. Anticipate an audience with your King, and rush not into his presence with the carelessness of one who goes only to an ordinary meal.

Nor would I array that sacred table with terrors to your mind. I am convinced, that many throw around the hallowed elements, a dread solemnity, which makes the timid and faltering believer feel, that if *he,* if one so vile as *he,* should touch them, he would eat and drink damnation to himself, and seal forever his hopelessness and his ruin. It was never the intention of our Lord, to hold up such fearful views of this feast of love. There is every thing about it that is inviting. It is a most pathetic appeal to the fearful and troubled soul. It woos, in silent but eloquent terms, the weary and heavy laden, to come and find rest. It is not Sinai—but Calvary. It is not the smoke, or the lightning, or the thunder—no, weak and mourning believer, it is the uplifted cross, and the expiring victim, whose blood speaks peace from every vein. Look on those significant, simple memorials—is there any terror in this scene? Is it not all peace, and love, and mercy?

The sacrament of the supper is a memorial of the love and compassion of Christ, a lively emblem of his suffering for sin. It is a public acknowledgement of our attachment to his cause. Having seriously and sincerely examined ourselves, and finding that we can humbly claim the characteristics of the true disciple, we may come to this feast of love, and commune with our Lord, and with one another, in a composed and humble frame of mind. If our greatest burden is sin, and our only ground of confidence is the Saviour, we have nothing to fear, but every thing to hope, from this delightful and affecting ordinance. Much of the profit of partaking of this sacrament, you will recollect, depends on your fidelity in the work of self-examination. If that be neglected, you have no reason to look for a blessing. If it be performed in a hurried and superficial manner, you need not expect much enjoyment in the ordinance. God will be glorified in them that make so near an approach to the mercy-seat.

When you approach the table, I would recommend it to you, to simplify your views as much as possible. By endeavouring to think of many things, the mind becomes confused. Having lifted your soul to God for light and feeling, look on the elements, and endeavour to view them as the appropriate memorials of your bleeding Lord. What do you see in that broken bread? Is it not the emblem of the mangled body of the Lamb of God? What meaneth that flowing wine? Is it not the emblem of the blood, which was shed for the remission of sins? And wherefore was that body broken, and that blood poured forth? O, my soul, let thy guilt and transgressions answer. Without the shedding of that blood, there had been no remission. What, then, can I render to my Lord, for all this dying love? I am speechless in gratitude. Here, blessed Saviour, I give thee all I have—this broken, contrite heart. Take it, O take it as thine own, wash it in thy blood, and seal it for thyself.

LETTER XXII.

On the subject of prayer and habitual self-examination, I shall add no more. You recollect, that I connected with these, as of equal importance, a close and diligent perusal of the scriptures. I shall therefore occupy your attention, for a short time, on this last mentioned topic.

The importance of making the word of God a devotional study, is evident, both from the testimony of that word, and the experience of all eminent saints who have ever lived. The more I study the sacred volume, the more deeply am I impressed with its magnificent glory, and its high importance to me as an accountable creature. Were I banished to a more lonely rock, than that inhabited by the Corsican exile, with my Bible I should only want food for the soul, and a stimulant to the understanding. I am astonished, that men of literature, of mere worldly wisdom, do not more frequently drink at this celestial fountain. Were they once to sip at this clear, pure stream, they could not but relish it. Such a relish, however, the Spirit alone can give.

It has charms, as a literary production, which the infidel has been constrained to acknowledge. Prejudice, not long since, had shut out these heavenly stores from many highly cultivated minds. The Bible was so common a book, and was so frequently found in the hands of the poor and the illiterate, that those who claimed to be learned and philosophic, took the liberty to despise it, and thus excluded themselves from the noblest source of mental and moral refinement. A young man, of irreligious character, who was a member of a respectable college, on hearing one of the professors refer to the beautiful comparison of our Saviour, when enjoining confidence in the providence of God, "Consider the lilies of the field, how they grow; they toil not neither do they spin; and yet I say unto you, that even Solomon, in all his glory, was not arrayed like one of these:"—turned to a fellow-student, and inquired where that striking and elegant language was found. On learning that it was found in the Bible, he was astonished. Have you never read your Bible? was the inquiry of his companion. "My Shakespeare," said he, "is all the Bible I ever read." This, I acknowledge, is an extreme case; but there are many similar to it. Even in our day, how little attention do the sacred oracles command!

While the shelf groans with destructive literature, and the mind rejoices in the same, the sublimities of the Law and the Prophecies; the tender, touching, simple narrations of Christ; the sublime devotional strains of "Israel's king;" the wisdom of the wisest man who ever lived; are regarded as dry and uninteresting. I cannot allow that man or woman, to possess even a cultivated or discriminating taste, who thus judges. I have read Homer and Milton; but when I compare their poetry to the lofty strains of David, Habakkuk, and Isaiah, it is the flickering light of a taper, to the flash of light of a thundercloud. I have read the pathetic story of Sterne, on the imprisoned criminal, and the melting appeal which Sir Walter puts into the mouth of a favourite heroine, when pleading in the royal presence for the life of her sister; but they are tame, when compared with the struggling emotions of a Joseph, and the short but heart-rending plea of his brother Judah.

But this comparison might be extended to the various departments of Bible literature. Its moral precepts, how concise, and yet how comprehensive? Its narrations seize on the most prominent and striking circumstances, without including any extra or unnecessary matter; and throughout, from Genesis to Revelation, there is an unearthly something, which stamps it as intelligence from the skies. Its analysis of character is wonderful. There is no other book on earth, in which there is so accurate, and full, and clear an exhibition of human nature.

But why am I comparing the Bible as a literary composition, to one who views this as its least attractive feature? Why have I wandered from the great point, of urging to an elevated standard of piety? Let us return, and view it as the great means of sanctification. "Sanctify them through thy truth," said our blessed Lord, "thy word is truth." This is the charm which so much attracts the pious heart. That heart is not insensible to the elegance of scriptural style, not indifferent to its bold and beautiful imagery; but these are not the principal attractions. It is the word of God. It reveals the way of salvation. It portrays the providence of God. It presents the Lamb of God slain for our transgressions. It communicates sweet strains of spiritual devotion. It brings into view a bright and eternal reward. It discloses the wounds of our nature, and offers the healing balm. In short, it embodies all that a Christian, in this pilgrimage, can need. It is his only chart through this tempestuous life. In trouble, it is his consolation; in prosperity, his monitor; in difficulty, his guide. Amid the darkness of death, and while descending into the shadowy valley, it is the day-star that illuminates his path, makes his dying eye bright with hope, and cheers his soul with the prospect of immortal glory.

Is this the book that vain and foolish minds undervalue and despise? From their folly, my young friend, learn thou a lesson of wisdom. Let your language be,

"May this blest volume ever lie
Close to my heart, and near mine eye;
Till life's last hour my soul engage,
And be my chosen heritage."

LETTER XXIII.

I WISH you never to forget, that the attainment of an elevated standard of piety, is intimately connected with a devoted and diligent reading of the scriptures. It is customary to recommend to the young Christian, various authors on practical piety. Such authors, I cordially unite in recommending; but I fear, that the youthful Christian, by too great an attention to disorderly reading, has sometimes given less attention to the Bible, than its primary importance demands.

Christians, in recommending such books, have taken it for granted, that the Bible is diligently and closely studied; but they have taken too much for granted. A taste for religious novelties has been excited, and the precious word has at length become comparatively uninteresting. If any book of mere human composition, be it ever so instructive, is to command more of our interest and attention than the Bible, we should, like Martyn, throw it aside, and reread the sacred volume, until we give it, in our hearts, its legitimate prominence and superiority.

When young Christians become devoted to this religious literature, the Bible is very apt to be neglected. They acquire a recklessness in discussing the superficial parts of Christianity; but I insist upon it, that they do not, by such reading, form a sound, consistent, and deeply spiritual character. Far be it from me to undervalue such reading. But I wish to impress upon your mind, the superiority of God's word. Other books of a religious character, should be considered as inferior to the Bible. When they throw light upon the sacred volume; when they drive you back to this great fountain of truth; when they quicken your diligence in studying it, and serve rather as hand-maids, than as rivals; they may be read with accuracy and with profit. But if you find that they draw away your interest from the word of God, and excite a taste for novelties, you must suspect them as competition, and immediately give again your highest affections to that precious book, to which they legitimately belong.

This caution is the more needful, because the press, at the present day, is filled with periodicals and works of fiction, which, bearing a slightly religious aspect, are considered as good substitutes for similar but irreligious books; and are therefore recommended to those whose consciences might revolt at the latter cast of productions. This furnishes a strong temptation to young Christians. I warn them against it. I would not restrict their reading entirely to the word of God. I would be far from prohibiting any merely innocent or instructive book. Let them be acquainted with poetry, history, etc., but I would guard against making this reading superior to the Bible. I believe there never can be an exalted Christian character, where the Bible is not made the first, and the best, and the most interesting of books. That person who cannot lay aside any volume, however interesting, for the Bible, and who cannot find in the latter, a greater relish than in the former, has never attained to an elevated standard of piety.

It has been said, that every thing in a minister's studies, should have a reference to the word of God. Through whatever fields of science, or of literature, he may rove, he should come back with superior relish to the Bible. The same advice should be given to the young Christian. In the varied regions of philosophy and taste, he is permitted to rove; but the Bible should be his richest banquet. Make it a rule always to prefer it. If at the hours of devotion, you are strongly drawn towards some new and interesting religious publication; if you are tempted to omit, for this, the regular study of the scriptures, regard it as a temptation, and resist it accordingly. You recollect the resolution of the pious Martyn, to which I have alluded. He never would allow himself to peruse a book one moment, after he felt it gaining a preference to his Bible. As long as he could turn to his Bible with a superior relish, so long he would continue reading, and no longer. Go thou and do likewise. If you commence with this resolution, you will find the advantages of it in your daily experience. The word of God will grow constantly in your estimation, and you will be ready to exclaim with David, "O how I love thy law; it is sweeter to my taste than honey, and the honeycomb."

My own experience convinces me, that the oftener and the more diligently you read the scriptures, the more beautiful will they appear, and the less relish will you have for light and superficial reading. There is, in an intimate acquaintance, in a daily conversation with the scriptures, something sanctifying, something ennobling. A satisfaction is felt in reading them, which no human composition can excite. You feel as if you were conversing with God and angels. You breathe a heavenly atmosphere. The soul is bathed in celestial waters. It drinks a sweetness and a composure, which shed over it unearthly attractions.

To this fountain of light and life, let us then daily resort. Here is the healing influence. Here is the pool of Bethesda. Here abounds consolation for the afflicted. Here hope dwells to cheer and to guide. "Bind this precious volume about your neck. Write it on the tablets of your heart." It will prove your shield in conflict, your guide in perplexity, your solace in adversity. When "death shall be swallowed up in victory," if it have been faithfully studied in this life, it will afford themes for heavenly contemplation through eternity.

LETTER XXIV.

It is a common practice, with young Christians, to confine their attention to certain parts of the scriptures, to the almost entire neglect of the rest. They select, generally, the devotional and preceptive portions, such as the Evangelists, the Psalms, and some of the Epistles. This circumstance, while it favours the evidence of their being Christians, is also best calculated, perhaps, to advance their growth in grace. In this early stage of their progress, they cannot be expected to take a comprehensive view of scriptural truth, and show a maturity of knowledge on doctrinal theology. But there is danger that this practice will be too long continued. If so, they will ever be children. They cannot grow in knowledge. They will be feeding on milk, when they ought to receive the more substantial food.

Permit me, therefore, my young friend, to caution you against undervaluing any part of the inspired volume. While I would rejoice in the fact of your having, at first, preferred those scriptures which are more particularly devotional, I must exhort you to go on to perfection. "All scripture is given by inspiration of God," and all is, therefore, profitable, for the attainment of that perfect standard, at which you aim.

In these remarks, I speak from personal experience. My attention, for a long time, was confined almost exclusively to the Psalms, the Evangelists, and a few of the plainest of the Epistles. These I read and reread, until much of them was committed to memory, and all were very familiar. I do not, nor shall I ever, regret this. But my mistake was, in supposing that the historical and prophetical, and some of the doctrinal parts of the Bible, were inapplicable to my circumstances, and therefore had little claim on my attention. I fear that others have fallen into this mistake. I have since learned that those very scriptures, to which I confined my attention, were greatly illuminated, and beautifully explained, by other parts of the Bible, which I had thought too deep, and too inapplicable for my reading.

The word of God is one magnificent whole. There is a oneness in all its proportions, and an harmonious measurement in all its parts. It is like a beautiful structure, built on the finest principles of architecture. The young Christian may be compared to a superficial observer, who is enraptured with a glance of the finely turned arches, and the highly finished columns of this temple. He dwells upon these, as the principal attractions. The more advanced saint, has not only entered the lobby, but has also penetrated the interior court. He has examined carefully the foundation, and admired its structure. He has found no part defective; no portion superfluous. As his mind sweeps in the noble pile at one glance, he exclaims, how magnificent! how grand! how worthy of the architect!

While, therefore, my young friend, I would encourage you, in reading closely those parts of the Bible, which appear most adapted to your character and circumstances, I would, at the same time, caution you not to neglect other important parts of sacred scripture. As I before observed, by reading the Bible as a whole, you will perceive much more clearly, the beauty of your favourite passages. The true method of interpreting scripture, is by comparing one part with another. Had I received and attended to this hint, my knowledge of scriptural truth would, I am persuaded, have been much more extensive than it is at present. I have learned from happy, though late experience, that the historical books of the Old Testament, not only throw light on all the subsequent inspired writings, but are filled with most exalted, and devotional, and soul-transporting sentiments. Since I began to study the scriptures in course, I have lingered on the Books of Moses, as on enchanted ground. The types and shadows have been full of meaning. In all of them, Christ and Him crucified, appears conspicuous.

I am convinced of the utility of studying the Bible in course; and I can assure you that my former unsettled practice, of opening and reading where the eye chanced to fall, was far from affording equal satisfaction. I note for your benefit, the circumstances which prevented my improvement in the knowledge of God's word, and I hope that you will carefully avoid them. You will find a solid satisfaction in studying the scriptures according to the mode I recommend. Consider it as the labour of life; for be assured, that should you live to the age of four-score years, you will not have attained perfection in this study. But why should I call it a labour, when it is so delightful a privilege? It is indeed a labour, to that being who loves not the character, and who yields not obedience to the law of God. But is it a labour to that mind which is attuned, by the Spirit's influence, to the beauties of celestial truth? Will not the soul expand under the developments of God, and of heavenly things?

As we learn more and more of the wisdom, the goodness, and the mercy of God, we shall the more fervently desire a conformity to these divine attributes. It is thus we shall grow in grace, and in the knowledge of God, and of our Saviour. In the visible creation, every thing is full of glory. Every thing speaks of the wisdom and the power of God, and invites the soul to ascend to its all-glorious Creator. But in the written word, we have God speaking to us without a medium, and speaking to us as to his children.

Go, then, my young friend, and diligently listen to the holy oracles. Search the scriptures. Peruse them systematically. Make them your daily and nightly companions. And may their celestial influence be so infused into your soul, that you shall progressively lose the image of the earthly, and assume the image of the heavenly inhabitants.

LETTER XXV.

You recollect, my young friend, that when speaking on the subject of prayer, I warned you against a hurried and superficial manner. I would repeat the same caution in respect to reading the Word of God. There is a careless, superficial attention to the Bible, which is neither acceptable to God, nor profitable to the soul.

We should ever approach that sacred Book with reverence. Though written by men, remember that those men "spake, as they were moved by the Holy Spirit." The medium through which it was communicated, detracts not from the divinity of the matter. When we open the sacred volume, we listen to the voice of God. It is the same voice, though unaccompanied by those terrific circumstances, which issued from that awful cloud which curtained the summit of Sinai. It is the same voice that was heard in such piteous lamentations from Calvary, when our Immanuel trode for us the wine press of the wrath of God. Should we not, therefore, give a reverential attention, when Jehovah speaks? Should not our posture be that of the deepest humility and awe?

When you take the scriptures in hand, it is well to let such a reflection pass your mind. It is profitable to pause a moment, and say within yourself, what a privilege do I enjoy in the reading of this sacred page? Millions of my fellow-beings are shut out from it. They have nothing but the dim and flickering light of nature. They are, therefore, degraded and besotted by ignorance and sensuality. Whereas, I am favoured with the clear light of revelation. I hold in my hand the mind and will of God concerning me. Are not my obligations, therefore, proportionately great? What account can I give at the judgment day, if I neglect or undervalue this precious volume? "O, Lord, open thou mine eyes, that I may behold wondrous things out of thy law." Unstop mine ear, that I may listen, and dispose my heart to receive and obey. Spirit of light! Inspirer of this heavenly book! Be present to dissipate my darkness, and shed over my soul the beams of celestial glory. Let me not fall under the condemnation of that wicked servant, who knew his master's will, but refused to perform it; but having, by thy illuminating influence, a perfect understanding of the word, may I, through thy sanctifying grace, be moulded by it, into the likeness and image of God.

I take it for granted that the study of the Bible, is to form a part of your daily devotions; and it is upon such a supposition, that I make these remarks. Beware, I entreat you, of the habit of glancing over different parts of the Bible, instead of reading it in course, and with close and diligent attention. The latter mode, accompanied with the blessing of God, will form an elevated Christian character. The former, is characteristic of the worldly-minded and superficial professor. Depend upon it, the closer attention you give the word, the more precious and interesting will it become, and the more rapidly will you grow in knowledge and holiness. The pious David, declared that his love for the word of God was so ardent, that it was his meditation day and night. I meditate, says he, on all thy precepts. I muse on the work of thy hands. It is this meditative spirit which I would recommend, when you are reading the scriptures.

Dr. Scott, as we learn from his memoirs, was in the habit of reading the Bible on his knees. Whenever a difficult part of divine truth came under consideration, he would lift his soul to God, for the illuminating influence of the Spirit. It was by prayer over the word of God, he formed a character that will stand as a bright example to all succeeding Christians. It was in this way, also, that he arrived at such a perfect knowledge of the scriptures, and was enabled to write his commentary. As you will need some help in studying the Bible, permit me here to recommend this admirable work.

I cannot do this better, than by copying a brief notice from the pen of a friend: "As an interpreter, he is clear, sober, and judicious. He never so dwells upon one doctrine, as to keep others out of view, (the grand defect of many expositors), but gives to each truth that proportion of notice which its relative importance seems to demand. The great doctrine of justification by faith alone, the very hinge on which the whole gospel turns, and its all-pervading principle, Dr. Scott very clearly and fully unfolds, where it is specially treated of in holy writ. He never loses sight of it upon any occasion, and uniformly so handles it, as to beat down the pride of the Pharisee on the one hand, and expose the corruption of the Antinomian on the other. But his commentary is not simply doctrinal; he shows all the varied bearings of the truth upon the inner and the outer man. In a word, he is highly experimental and practical throughout. And for this part of his work, he appears peculiarly competent. Never, perhaps, were displayed in any uninspired composition, such a deep insight into the natural workings of the human heart, and so accurate a knowledge of the exercises of a mind renewed by divine grace; combined with such an enlarged, and at the same time minute acquaintance with human life, under every variety of circumstance. To write this work, demanded such observation of the world, united to such studious habits, as could very rarely indeed be found in the same individual. And the Lord seems to have led this man through just the path that would qualify him to compose such a book."

I can add my agreement to the above. It will be found, I believe, that his opinion on all important points, is the correct one. I must conclude, therefore, by advising you to commence his work with a determination, by the blessing of God, to finish it. Prospectively, it may appear a task; but be assured, it is not. As you advance, you will find each succeeding page, more and more delightful.

LETTER XXVI.

I HOPE, my young friend, that you will acquire a thorough acquaintance with the historical scriptures. They are intimately connected with the prophetical, the doctrinal, and the preceptive parts of the Bible. I have, at times, been made to blush for my ignorance of some fact, which has been referred to, as a part of Bible history and especially as quoted by the New Testament writers; not because I neglected the Bible, but because I confined my reading to a very limited portion of it.

It is impossible to understand the prophecies, without a knowledge of the sacred history. It is equally impossible, without this knowledge, to comprehend the beauty and force of the gospels and the epistles. The more thoroughly you study the Old, the more easily will you comprehend the meaning and beauty of the New Testament. If you will become intimately acquainted with the Book of Leviticus, the Epistle to the Hebrews will possess charms which you had never attributed to it. If you have discriminated between the covenant which God made with Abraham, and that which He formed with the people of Israel, at Sinai, you will be prepared to estimate the force of the Apostle's reasoning, in the Epistle to the Galatians. There is scarcely any part of the New

Testament, which has not some connexion with the Old. In the historical books, you have also an exhibition of the providence of God, and many bright examples of patriarchal Christianity. You cannot fail, therefore, of being amply rewarded by a diligent reading of the sacred history.

In studying the doctrinal parts of the Bible, you will require much patience and perseverance, mingled with constant prayer for heavenly illumination. There is reason to apprehend, that many young Christians have vague and superficial notions of the doctrines, whilst they exhibit much of the true temper of the gospel. If, however, they neglect to investigate and understand the doctrines of scripture, they will be in danger of being led astray, by the seducing influence of heresy. Be well grounded, therefore, in the fundamental doctrines of the Bible. In making up your opinion with respect to any doctrine, avoid a rash and hasty conclusion. Be deliberate, and you will escape the imputation of "being carried about with every wind of doctrine." When a truth, which you have thus deliberately embraced, is called in question, be not induced by the apparent sincerity, or the worthy arguments of your opponent, to yield your opinion, until you have given it a thorough investigation. You may still be right, and your opponent wrong. Be not rash in giving up *your* opinion and adopting *his*. This caution is perhaps necessary to young Christians, who cannot, at their age, be supposed to be thoroughly indoctrinated.

There are some truths which you have received from education. I would advise you to re-examine them, by the word of God, and if they correspond therewith, to hold them fast, as the most precious legacy which your pious parents have bequeathed. It will be insinuated, perhaps, that such opinions are the result of education, and are destitute of any other foundation. Be cautious in admitting this. Search the scriptures, and if you find them there, hold them fast, as a "form of sound words." If they are opposed to the Bible, abandon them, however dear, or sanctified by parental affection. But in yielding such opinions, I would still say, be not rash. Investigate closely and sincerely before you let them go. There is a tenderness of conscience in young Christians, which Satan sometimes pushes to a painful and distressing embarrassment. This is as much the case in respect to belief, as to external conduct.

As an illustration of these remarks, there occurs to my recollection, the case of a youth, who, on making a public profession of religion, joined, as a matter of course, the church in which he had been baptized, and to which his parents belonged. For a short time all went happily with him. He enjoyed the communion of the saints, and the ordinances of the gospel. The scene, however, was soon changed. His mind was thrown into great distress, by the insinuations of one, who, by his bold and dogmatical mode of reasoning, led him into doubts on a particular point of doctrine. He was deeply perplexed as to the path of duty. At one time, the adversary would suggest the guilt of remaining a day longer in his present connexion. At another, he would insinuate that he had made a false profession, and therefore had committed the sin against the Holy Ghost. In this hour of anguish, he prayed most earnestly for direction. The thought occurred to him, that he need not be rash in altering his views. As he was comparatively a child, and had much to learn, God would not be displeased, if he took time for investigation. This thought gave him consolation, and he set about a diligent and prayerful examination of the Bible. The result was, a conviction of the truth as he had held it, and a perfectly settled state of mind on that point, even to the present time.

I hope, therefore, my young friend, that in

making up your doctrinal opinions, you will study the word of God closely and prayerfully. Be careful not to rush into hasty conclusions from isolated passages; but take a comprehensive view of the connexion. Look at the Bible in all its grand and magnificent proportions. Be thoroughly indoctrinated, and you will become a growing and stable Christian. There will be a solidity in your character, which, like a foundation that is well adjusted to the superstructure, will be, at once, the evidence, both of permanency and of beauty.

LETTER XXVII.

I would not, my young friend, have you study the Bible as a critic; but as a Christian. You should endeavour to derive some spiritual nourishment from every part of scripture. In this, Dr. Scott's commentary is well recommended to assist you. In studying the historical Scriptures, you can occasionally pause and meditate. You can inquire, whether your mind distinctly comprehended the facts recorded, and their practical bearing. In this way, your memory will be strengthened, and your heart, I trust, often affected.

Before I leave this subject, permit me to say a word or two, on the spirit with which you should read the sacred volume. It is a spirit of sincere faith, and child-like obedience. There are many parts of scripture, which, after the most diligent and careful investigation, will still appear, to short-sighted man, almost unexplainable. There are many doctrines too deep for human comprehension—many mysterious truths relating to God, to angels, and to heaven. God has given to man a revelation, which embodies the majestic truths of eternity, and of his infinite attributes; which brings into view a spiritual world, and throws down upon us the light of the inconceivable glory; and such a revelation must necessarily contain things to us mysterious and incomprehensible. It necessarily presents certain truths to be received on the simple testimony of God; and this is faith. Shall I, therefore, in reading the Bible, reject one of its doctrines, because it is less intelligible than another? Am I not bound to receive even incomprehensible truths, if I find them there recorded? Having settled the fact, that the Bible is inspired, I must come to it, as to an infallible oracle. I must feel, with the apostle, that although there are many things, which, in consequence of my infirmity, I can only view as through a glass darkly; yet, if I am a Christian, the time is near, when I shall see them as clearly as I can behold a friend face to face. Although I must confess, that there are many deep truths which now I know but in part, yet there is a day coming, when I shall know them as fully, as I myself am known. Even the venerable apostle ranks himself but as a child in the knowledge of divine things. He is content to wait until that knowledge shall be expanded among the bright intelligences of heaven.

Were your father, whom you so much love, a scientist, familiar with the motions of the heavenly bodies; were he to take you, while a child, to his observatory; point you to those revolving orbs; and tell you that he had measured their distances, and calculated their motions: would you believe him? O yes; he is your father, who would not deceive you, and you are his confiding child. You could not comprehend the fact; but you would believe your father; you would have no doubt of his truth. Were he again to tell you, that, should your life be continued, you also would in a few years, be able to make these exalted calculations; your astonishment would be increased. Had not your father said it, you could not have believed it. But still you would confide in your beloved parent.

This is precisely the spirit which you must possess in studying the scriptures. It is your Father who speaks. Sometimes he speaks of high and mysterious things; but remember that you are bound to confide in His word. When skepticism would harass your mind, flee to the word of God, and subject your understanding implicitly to its dictates. When troubles assail, betake yourself, instantly, to this fountain of consolation. When doubts of your acceptance come over your mind like a dark cloud, here, in this blessed volume, is the sun of righteousness to chase away the cloud, and restore you to calmness and tranquillity.

Whilst there is a spirit abroad that would undervalue the plain testimony of revelation, and make it, like the heathen oracles of old, speak a doubtful and time-serving language, be it your resolution to cling to the precious Bible, and to love even its most self-denying and soul-humbling doctrines. Be not ashamed of those views of truth, which, in the estimation of vain and proud man, are peculiar only to vulgar minds. The Bible, you will recollect, was written equally for the vulgar and the refined. The poor claim it as their most precious legacy. What though there be in it some mysterious and unexplainable doctrines; is it not the part of faith, to sit meekly at the Saviour's feet, and receive implicitly the words which drop from his lips?

Compassed about as we are with infirmities; dependent as we are for the least ray of heavenly comfort; with intellectual pride on the one hand, and deep-rooted and sinful prejudices on the other; now wandering from God and duty, and now returning disappointed and dejected; let us sink into the deepest self-abasement. Let us bow with the spirit of children, to the simple truth as it is in Jesus: let us implore the Divine Spirit to guide us through this dark desert; and let us look forward by faith to the period when we shall emerge from our darkness, into unclouded and eternal day.

LETTER XXVIII.

By this time, my young friend, you perceive that religion is the business of life; a momentous work, which will task every faculty to the utmost. To make a profession in the visible church, is one thing; but to prove, by a progressive improvement in knowledge and holiness, our connexion with the church invisible, is another. When I look around and behold so many youth gathered within the church, by the sanctifying influence of the numerous and powerful revivals of religion, my soul exults in the prospective glories of our Zion. These, methinks, are the generations who are to urge forward the cause of Christ, and who may be permitted to chant the jubilee of Millenial glory.

I am anxious, that the rising generation of Christians should assume a more elevated standard of piety and action, than that which has characterized their predecessors; and that primitive holiness, and generosity, and self-denial, should once more appear, as the earnest pledge of that glorious completion, when holiness shall be inscribed, even on the hearts of men. I confess, however, that I have my misgivings. I have seen some, who but lately gave favorable promise of this high and noble character, sinking down to the dead level of ordinary professors, taking the character of those around them, and appearing contented with just so much religion as will render them agreeable to all, without incurring the censure of any. How unworthy of a great and noble character! I would never lay my hand upon the sacred covenant, or I would lay along with it my *heart,* my full, free, undivided heart.

The gospel of Christ admits of no compromise. It demands our all. If it required less, it would be unworthy of its great author and finisher. I rejoice that it requires all. This is its glory. When we are brought to yield to its claims, and give up all, then, and not till then, will it throw around us its arms of mercy. And what *is* our all? What do we give, when we give our all? A polluted soul, that might justly be cast into hell; a body, the miserable companion of that soul, and groaning under the dire effects of disobedience and guilt. Our all consists, at last, in nothing more than a polluted and guilty nature.

What a wonder is it, that God will accept such an offering! What a miracle of mercy, that raises us up from our pollution, bathes us in the washing of regeneration, and clothes us in the white linen of the saints! And do we talk about self-denial? Do we say, how hard to give up all? I am ashamed to use such language; ashamed to hear it used. What did Christ give up for us? Let that question blot out "self-denial," from the Christian's vocabulary. When you think the gospel makes severe requirements, by requiring all, go up to Mount Calvary, and weep over such suggestions. See the blood of your Immanuel so freely gushing from a heart that never exercised towards you any emotion but love; love unspeakable—love unsought—and love for the guilty. Go hide your head in shame and penitence, at such a thought. It is a glorious privilege, my young friend, to give up all to Christ. The soul that feels the constraining influence of his love, asks not how little may be given, consistently with obtaining the heavenly reward; asks not for the lowest standard of discipleship; it burns with an ardent desire to devote all, and to aim at perfect "conformity to his death."

It is sad, to behold so many satisfied with a name in the church, and a seat at the sacramental board. This appears to make up the sum of their religion. Others go one step farther, and observe some decent regard to what may be termed an experiment in religion; but aim not at that elevated standard which it is their privilege to attain. They live in doubt, and they often die in darkness. They enjoy neither religious consolations, nor the peace which the world giveth. All this is in consequence of the miserable, half-way, compromising spirit, which seeks to perform the service, and enjoy the approval, of two masters.

Let me entreat you to make a noble surrender in this cause. The world has hitherto been the master, and you must acknowledge, that you have rendered a full and faithful service; but shall you yield a less free and faithful devotion to Christ? Which is the more worthy of your regard? Which has the greater claims on your affections? Which offers the fullest reward? Determine by the grace of God, that you will forsake all and follow Christ; do not, like Peter, follow him afar off, but, like Mary, sit at his feet; like the beloved disciple, rest upon his bosom.

You will perceive from my communications thus far, that there is work enough to do; that there is some struggling for the prize; that you are not to sit down and idly imagine that now you have joined the church, there remaineth no more for you to do; that you are to be carried along, as it were, by a sort of invisible influence to heaven, without any extraordinary exertions of your own. Determine, that if others act on the principles of the spiritual sluggard, you will leave them, and march forward towards the elevation of Christian character, which the Bible plainly marks out as your duty and your privilege. Onward, is the daily watchword of the faithful soldier of the cross. He sleeps not at his post. He hears the first note of alarm, and prepares for the conflict. He loves his King, and obedience is a pleasure, rather than a duty.

O may you aim high, in contending for the prize of your high calling! May you go from strength to strength, from victory to victory, from one attainment to another, until you shall stand, a glorious example on earth; until you shall inherit the highest rewards of the blessed in heaven!

CONCLUSION.

THE duties which I have been urging upon you, as important in forming an elevated standard of piety, are those especially which relate to God, and your own soul. Social obligations, and the relative duties of life, I have not considered. They are not first in importance. Besides, if you give heed to the advice which I have presented in these sheets; if you persevere in the path which I have marked out; if you give the diligence in prayer, in self-examination, and the study of the Bible, which I have urged; you will, most certainly, not be a delinquent, in the various social and domestic duties of life.

The course recommended, if faithfully pursued, will have a controlling influence upon your intercourse with others. It will put every thing in its proper place, and give every duty its legitimate prominency and attention. It will make you the obedient child, the beloved sister, the diligent scholar, and the amiable and intelligent companion.

I cannot believe, my young friend, that the serious cautions, solemn warnings, and earnest appeals, which I have made, are to be entirely lost. I flatter myself, that when the hand which penned, and the heart which prompted them, are silent in the grave; she, for whose instruction they were given, will exhibit all that maturity of knowledge, all that purity of character, all that holy elevation of purpose and of action, which together constitute the fulness of Christian perfection. But if, after all, you should make a compromise with the world, and be willing to settle down upon that low and unworthy standard, too common among our churches; if a few years should find you foremost in pleasure and in fashion, and undistinguished from the noisy, vain, and trifling crowd; methinks your conscience will have been rapidly seared, and your heart quickly steeled to a sense of your duty.

But I am persuaded better things of you, though I thus speak. Still, I know more, than you can at present, of the deceitfulness of the heart, the subtle insinuations of Satan, and the powerful attractions which the world presents to a warm, youthful imagination. Secluded as you now are, you can form but a faint conception, of the power of worldly seductions. Perhaps you are ready to conclude, that your heart is impregnable to all their assaults. This, be assured, is a great mistake. Think not that your mountain stands strong. If you indulge this thought, you will most assuredly fall; you will be obliged to weep over the disgrace which you will have brought upon religion; you will, perhaps, be constrained to bewail the ruin of some soul, who may have been emboldened in sin, through your carelessness or heedlessness. You have a dangerous road to travel. You cannot be too vigilant; you cannot offer too many prayers for guidance and protection. Your armour cannot be too bright, nor your eye too cautious.

Remember what I have already said, that declension begins at the closet. Watch there, for its first appearance. There, be ready to discover and to correct it. Prayer is your strong hold. In every dark, distressful hour, cast an eye upward to God. When the world displays its fascination, and woos you away to its arms, God, and God alone, is the "strength of your heart." When afflictions come, and the soul is made sad and desolate, where then shall you look, but to Him who heareth the mourner's cry? Prayer has ever been powerful and efficient. It has wiped away the tear of the penitent, and lighted up the gleam of hope. It has broken the stout sinews of rebellion, and transformed the lion to the lamb.

In the work of self-examination, be close and thorough; be habitual and persevering. Let a nice discrimination run through your investigations. Remember your aim. It is high; it is the elevated character. Deal faithfully then with your own soul. Severely judge it, from the law of God. Anticipate the great and final account. It will then not burst upon you unprepared. You will go calmly forward to the bar of God, and unhesitatingly open your bosom, conscious of forgiveness, to his keen inspection.

Let the word of God dwell in your heart. Study its sacred pages with prayerful diligence, and bow to its doctrines with implicit faith. Be it the man of your counsel; the guide of your belief; the foundation of your hope.

In short, take to yourself the whole armour of God; the shield of faith, by which you may quench the fiery darts of Satan; the helmet of salvation, to adorn and defend your head; the breastplate of righteousness, to cover your bosom from the shafts of slander or of envy; the sword of the Spirit, whose keen edge will make you resolute and fearless in the attack, powerful and irresistible in the defence. Thus arrayed, look upward, and press onward. God is your strength; and when He nerves the arm, though it be the arm of the weakest believer, that arm is irresistible. Lay not aside your weapons, while one foe within is unsubdued, or one enemy without unconquered. But life is short. The time is at hand, when you shall have a full and free discharge.

The crown of glory glitters in prospect. After a few more days of obedience to your King, that crown shall be placed upon your brow.

When death comes, he will prove your last enemy. As he falls beneath your triumphant struggle, you shall hear the notes of victory, bursting from ten thousand angels on your dying ear. Then your work is done. Then your warfare is over. On yonder heavenly plains, you shall receive a golden harp, and learn celestial music. You shall sound that name by which you conquered; and in your eternal song, chant the praise of Him, who sitteth upon the throne, and of the Lamb forever. The trials of life will be remembered no more, or if remembered, will serve as new themes of praise and thanksgiving.

What a consummation! Who would not struggle a few short days, to inherit so rich a reward—to wear forever so bright a diadem?